FLIRTING — HOW TO DO IT

What better way is there to start a relationship than to flirt? In this innovative book you'll learn the fine art of relating to others and attracting them to you, and you'll soon be making connections—instead of excuses. Expert flirt Susan Rabin will teach you:

- ❤ How to make eye contact and the "flirting triangle" work for you
- ❤ How to master the five "W's" of (not-so) small talk
- ❤ The best way to start and end a good conversation
- ❤ How to make techniques like the "echo," the "third ear," and the "three R's" work for you
- ❤ How to turn self-denial and self-destruction into self-esteem and self-support
- ❤ The best way to handle the sting of rejection and get back in the saddle
- ❤ How to end a relationship with Mr. or Ms. Not-Quite-Right and still respect yourself in the morning.

HOW TO ATTRACT ANYONE, ANYTIME, ANYPLACE

SUSAN G. RABIN, M.A., former Family Living/Sex Education Coordinator for the New York City Board of Education, is a therapist, speaker, and workshop leader. She gives frequent lectures at Canyon Ranch Spa, the Learning Annex, and the Discovery Center. She has appeared on radio and television, including "The Montel Williams Show," Lifetime cable network's "Attitudes," and "Good Day New York." She lives in New York City.

SUSAN RABIN
WITH BARBARA LAGOWSKI

HOW TO
ATTRACT
ANYONE,
ANYTIME,
ANYPLACE

THE SMART GUIDE
TO FLIRTING

A PLUME BOOK

PLUME

Published by the Penguin Group
Penguin Books USA Inc., 375 Hudson Street, New York, New York 10014, U.S.A.
Penguin Books Ltd, 27 Wrights Lane, London W8 5TZ, England
Penguin Books Australia Ltd, Ringwood, Victoria, Australia
Penguin Books Canada Ltd, 10 Alcorn Avenue, Toronto, Ontario, Canada M4V 3B2
Penguin Books (N.Z.) Ltd, 182-190 Wairau Road, Auckland 10, New Zealand

Penguin Books Ltd, Registered Offices:
Harmondsworth, Middlesex, England

First published by Plume, an imprint of Dutton Signet,
a division of Penguin Books USA Inc.

First Printing, October, 1993
12   14   16   18   20   19   17   15   13   11

Portions of this book first appeared in Complete Woman and Cosmopolitan.

REGISTERED TRADEMARK—MARCA REGISTRADA

LIBRARY OF CONGRESS CATALOGING IN PUBLICATION DATA
Rabin, Susan.
How to attract anyone, anytime, anyplace : the smart guide to flirting / by Susan
Rabin with Barbara Lagowski.
p.   cm.
ISBN 0-452-27086-3
1. Man-woman relationships. 2. Interpersonal attraction. 3. Etiquette.
I. Lagowski, Barbara J. II. Title.
HQ801.R14   1993
306.7—dc20
93-10133
CIP

Printed in the United States of America
Set in Century Expanded and Kabel

Designed by Steven N. Stathakis

BOOKS ARE AVAILABLE AT QUANTITY DISCOUNTS WHEN USED TO PROMOTE PRODUCTS OR
SERVICES. FOR INFORMATION PLEASE WRITE TO PREMIUM MARKETING DIVISION, PEN-
GUIN BOOKS USA INC., 375 HUDSON STREET, NEW YORK, NEW YORK 10014.

This book is dedicated to the salmon who swim upstream, and my loving family and friends who helped me with my struggle. I hope I can help others with theirs.

ACKNOWLEDGMENTS

To my mom and dad. I wish they could read this book, but I am sure they know of my happiness and success, and I want to thank them for giving me the intelligence, personality, ability to persevere, and education so that I could make this book happen.

To my three children, Stuart, Jeff, and Frannie, who kept me on my toes as a single parent, and gave me a reason to work hard and persist and above all a desire to learn to love well. They taught me lessons of life not found in the school books, ones that only experience and motherhood can provide. Sometimes raising children alone felt like an endless struggle, but one well worth it, and I am very proud of each of them. They turned out to be exceptional grown-ups.

To my sister, Jewel, whose name only begins to describe her precious qualities. She is loved and appreciated in ways words cannot express, and was always there for me. I thank God she will read this book and enjoy my successes with me.

To the best sister-in-law a person could have, Laura. Never too busy or tired to listen (and listen well) to my ramblings. I hope to fulfill my promise to her yet. Laura, the chauffeur is on the way, she's just a little late.

To my brother, a real treat of a guy who taught me early what a good man and loving brother is, and gave me my first inkling of how different men are from women, and just how okay that is.

To Ben, my brother-in-law to whom I owe my sense of humor and love of sports. He is a very good man and made me feel special and cared for especially when the chips were down.

To my dear friends:

Lynn, so kind, supportive, and loyal from the first lecture she attended through all our ups and downs. Here come the good times, Lynn, enjoy them with me.

Rosemary, who laughed with me all the way through our writing conferences as we learned our craft, and encouraged and edited my work at all times of day and night. Thanks for being there, Rosemary.

Claire, my author friend whom I admired and tried to emulate, and who always insisted that I could write this book when I didn't think it possible. She was there personally and professionally to keep me going. Thanks, Claire.

Dolores, a dear friend whose talent inspired me to keep on going because she told me *I* had talent, and I thought *she* must know, as she hung in there to advise me. Thanks, Dee.

Herb, who introduced me to my agent Sandra, because everytime we talked he said, "You have great ideas, do something about them."

To Sandra, an agent sent from heaven. She believed in my book, and made everyone else believe in it too, and used her natural flirting ability and charm to get this book to publication.

To Peter, my friend and editor, with whom instant rapport was easy. Thanks, Peter, for the belief, confidence, and skill you gave to me and this book to make this project as exciting a reality as it is.

To Barry, the man I most love to flirt with and have for many years. Thank you, Barry, for your astuteness as my attorney, and making my life a pleasure, personally and professionally. Besides, any man who can finish the Sunday *Times* crossword puzzle in half an hour and lets me think I'm good at it too, is a gentlemen worth loving.

To the men in my life, thanks for enjoying me as a woman and letting me practice my flirting and relating skills which helped me to become who I am today and taught me to love and be loved in a healthy way.

To Dr. Albert Ellis, whose professional training helped me grow personally and professionally and enabled me to help others do the same.

To all my friends and relatives who are not mentioned personally, but know who you are. Thank you for touching my life and caring about me. I have learned and loved with you.

To the men and women who have attended my seminars and lectures—my friends and clients. You are who inspired me to write this book. I am so glad you were willing to come to the workshops and lectures to learn and to share your experiences. I gained much from you as well. I hope this book will further help you achieve what you desire, always.

To the children, teenagers, and teachers I have taught and guided in health and sex education for the New York City Board of Education. Thanks for the opportunity to make a difference in your lives. I hope this book will guide you further and increase your insights in the future.

To Miss Johnson, my eighth grade English teacher,

who taught me an appreciation of the English language and the writers who used it so well. She may never know of her influence, but like all great teachers she inspired me. When she wrote in my autograph book at graduation, "A thing of beauty is a joy forever" (Keats), I just knew she meant me, and that was the foundation for my positive self-esteem.

And to a nameless woman who delivered a speech at a health education conference in 1959, "The Gift of Greatness," in which she told her audience, "We as women truly had the gift of greatness, as we sacrificed by leaving our loved ones for the weekend to enhance our education." I waited a long time and took a circuitous path, as many women of my generation did, but I found my way toward doing what I felt destined for and her words never left me.

Lastly, to the salmon that swim upstream to spawn. I know how hard that journey is, but I am happy to say "I made it!"

CONTENTS

IF ALL YOU'RE
LOOKING FOR AT THE
LAUNDROMAT
IS AN AVAILABLE
DRYER . . . LOOK AGAIN!

Bus stops. Hardware stores. Dog runs. Box-office lines. Business meetings. Grocery stores. To most busy singles, these are nothing more than time-consuming stop-offs en route to the parties, dances, and bars where they hope to meet that certain someone. But to the thousands of adventurous, available men and women who have adopted my philosophy—that you can attract anyone, anytime, anyplace—the bakery is a local hot spot. (Where else can you flirt with the tantalizing idea of éclairs for lunch as well as the possibility of having dinner with that attractive customer beside you?) The office-supply store isn't just a place to buy that new date book—it's an opportunity to fill it in. Even a visit to the neighborhood laundromat doesn't have to be a social wash. (In fact, one of my single friends met a

man over Clorox who put her into a very enjoyable whirl—
for more than five years!)

The jogging track, deli counter, self-service gas station
... these may not seem like the most romantic places in the
world. But *anyplace* you meet that special someone becomes a special place to you. Best of all, no matter which
field you play (or how long you've played it!) you *can* meet
and attract new and interesting men and women everywhere you go. You just have to know what to do when you
get there.

FLIRTING AND THE FINE ART OF SOCIAL INTERCOURSE

Social intercourse. What an icebreaker! I've been single,
married, and single again, and I'm here to say that some of
the most satisfying intercourse I've had has been the discourse that takes place within the first five minutes of
meeting a new person. Of course I don't mean physical re-
lations. That kind of irresponsible behavior went out when
more than twenty-one kinds of sexually transmitted diseases came in. But social intercourse—that exciting
meeting of the minds that turns virtual strangers into fascinating friends (or lovers)—can be better than sex. For
one thing, you can do it anywhere. For another, you can
seek it as many times a day as you want, provided you
know how to flirt.

"FLIRT" IS NOT A DIRTY WORD

Contrary to what your mother may have told you, "flirt" is
not a five-letter synonym for all those four-letter words
that mean "tease." Flirting is a charming and honest expression of interest in another person. It is never coquettish or coy. (Drop a handkerchief in the street these days
and all you'll get is a dirty hanky!) Flirting isn't even
quaintly old-fashioned. In fact *conversation* has become the

preferred form of sexuality in the '90s. Flirting is a safe, intriguing way to get to hello and beyond.

Lucky for me, I have always been a natural flirt. I speak whether or not I am spoken to—and I take it like a trooper when no one speaks back. I approach others if they don't approach me. And I can make conversation with a blank wall if need be. (And what single person hasn't found himself or herself across a dinner table from one of those?)

On the personal level, my ability to flirt has enabled me to communicate my feelings and understand the signals of others. Over the years, these skills have led me to marriage, shaken me out of the doldrums of divorce, and provided me with a constant supply of fascinating, creative companions.

And because flirting has everything to do with communication, it has enhanced my professional life as well. Nonsexual flirting has helped me to become a more effective therapist, a successful lecturer, a popular television guest, and, through New York's Discovery Center and Learning Annex, the leader of my own standing-room-only seminars on (what else?) how to attract anyone, anytime, anyplace.

CAN *YOU* LEARN TO FLIRT?

Of course you can! Flirting is no more difficult than dancing *if* you learn the proper steps—and *if* you stop skipping the ones you think you don't need!

Since 1985, I have shown thousands of single men and women how to make that all-important first move, how to turn that first move into a first date, and how to use flirting skills to enhance every aspect of their lives. And their successes have been my successes. Of the 2,500 "graduate flirts" who have attended my lectures or enrolled in my seminars, virtually all have reported an increase in social activity, sharper communication skills, and the self-confidence to speak to and attract whomever they want, wherever they are. Many who have adopted my belief that the key to Attracting Anyone, Anytime, Anyplace is Approach, Attitude, and Action have found that special someone and have since taken themselves out of the singles market.

As the song goes, "It's a wonderful world, full of beautiful people." And my strategies for meeting the opposite sex will open up that world for you. Whether you are shy or merely inexperienced, the simple techniques in this book will enable you to approach new contacts with confidence, to communicate with them (often without saying a word!) and to interpret their messages in return. And whether you are happily single or actively looking, this invaluable guide provides you with all the skills you need to date, relate, or meet your mate, including how to converse with anyone about anything; how to use provocative props; what the ability to listen says about you; and how to give feelings of rejection the big brush-off. As you read this book, refrain from viewing the word *flirt* as a noun, and try to think of it as a verb. When someone says, "He/she is a flirt!" the noun sounds pejorative and may label the person as a tease, manipulator, or insincere. As a verb, flirt or flirting connotes action—being playful, friendly, conversant, and charming. It has a "zen" quality, by living in and enjoying the moment without thought of the outcome. To flirt allows you to act and interact *without* serious intent as you successfuly meet and relate to others.

Some enchanted evening, might *you* meet a stranger across a crowded folding table? Who knows? But I can assure you of this: if you can flirt, your life—and laundromats—will never be the same!

To you, I give *permission to flirt*. It is okay to flirt! In fact, it is *more* than okay; it is *necessary* in the '90s in getting to know someone, and is the first positive step for attracting anyone, anytime, anyplace!

1

REDISCOVERING
THE FLIRT IN YOU

You may not know it. You may not be sure you like it. But there's a flirt in you. And whether that alter ego is shy or gregarious, bold or bashful, it makes itself known everywhere you go, with everyone you meet.

To become the best flirt you can be, it's imperative that you get to know the kind of flirt you already are. Because this quiz reveals your social strengths and weaknesses, it will give you a head start on first-class flirting. And because your quest for an effective flirting style must be compatible with your quest for a significant other, the pointers you learn here can set you apart from the crowd.

Ready to come face to face with the flirt you are? Take out a pencil and get started. What you find may surprise you.

1. You're at a local diner and you spot a drop-dead gorgeous guy or gal at the counter. You
   A. hide behind your newspaper and keep your eyes focused on the print, wishing but never daring to make eye contact.
   B. find an article that allows you to expound on your own viewpoints and begin a conversation with the intriguing stranger.
   C. immediately take stock of his or her physical attributes. What a bod!
   D. assess the person's possibilities and decide to pass. He or she is just not your type.
   E. gush, "What a bright, sunny smile you have! It positively lights up the room!" Compliments always work.
   F. do nothing. Relationships with people you meet on the street are dangerous . . . and they never work out anyway.
   G. think of a million great opening lines—and imagine how the person might respond to each of them.

2. You think flirting is
   A. silly, contrived, and manipulative.
   B. a great way for people to get to know you.
   C. something you have to do to get sex.
   D. something you have to do to get married.
   E. easy if you just tell people what they want to hear.
   F. a technique that works only if you're one of the beautiful people and lucky in love.
   G. a nerve-racking pastime. The result is so hard to predict.

3. The conversation you are having with a new prospect begins to lag. You handle the situation by
   A. excusing yourself. If this person can't think of anything to ask you about, she or he obviously doesn't find you interesting.

B. revealing some fascinating tidbit about yourself.

C. telling a suggestive joke. You know a million of them!

D. finding a new conversational partner. This one is obviously not for you.

E. feigning ignorance about a subject in which your new friend shows expertise. Making the other person feel smart is good flirting!

F. saying nothing. It doesn't do much for the conversation, but it beats saying the wrong thing.

G. wondering what the other person is thinking. If you could only get into his or her brain!

4. At the local market, you notice an attractive shopper squeezing the melons. You also notice that he or she isn't wearing a wedding ring. You

A. make it a policy never to talk to strangers. Too bad, too. This one is awfully appealing!

B. walk right over and announce, "I'm a pro at selecting melons!" Then you shove an appropriate one into his or her hand and say, "Here—try this one."

C. can't wait to try out that cute melon line! If you're a woman, you hold one in each hand and ask, "How do you like these honeydews?" If you are a man, you sidle up and say, "Oh, I don't know. *Your* melons look pretty good to me."

D. walk on by. If this person doesn't know how to select fruit, he or she'll never fit into your healthy lifestyle.

E. ask him or her to help *you* choose melons! All that squeezing and knocking is so confusing!

F. move on to the next aisle. Anyone who's that careful about produce has got to be hyperfastidious, perfectionistic, or married, ring or no ring.

G. can't decide what to do so you circle the fruit counter hoping the stranger will notice you.

5. At a dinner party, you catch sight of a guest you suspect might be the man or woman of your dreams. You'd love to chat him or her up over dinner. You
A. wait until everyone is seated at the table, then take the only remaining chair. You don't want to seem obvious. Besides, pushy people are unattractive.
B. corner the object of your flirtation at the bar, then follow him or her to the table, positioning your body so that nobody else could possibly get close.
C. walk behind him or her to the table, then whisper invitingly in his or her ear: "Sit down. I think I love you."
D. wonder why he or she passed up the Thai beef appetizer. Is he or she a vegetarian? Vegetarians can be so dogmatic.
E. pour on the compliments like gravy. What a dish!
F. seat yourself as far as you can from this very special guest. What could you possibly have to say to such a perfect person?
G. wander around the room until you come up with just the right opening line. By the time you do, you notice that someone else has taken the seat you'd hope to get.

This quiz is quick and easy to score. Just circle the letter before each answer that comes closest to yours, then count up how many answers of the same letter you have marked. Is there a preponderance of one type of answer? Then you will definitely find yourself in the descriptions below. If your answers are split, read each of the appropriate paragraphs. The tips you'll find there will give you some real insight on dating and relating to the opposite sex. And insight is what real flirting "style" is all about.

THE "I DON'T FLIRT" FLIRT

"Flirting is manipulative," Mary told me during her first counseling session with me. "I simply will not come on to men. Why should I? Men have names for girls who do."

If you answered A to most of the quiz questions, you are ambivalent about making your availability known—and may be stuck in a negative mind-set about what flirting is and is not.

Contrary to Mary's opinion, you can take a pass on coquettish behavior without allowing attractive prospects to pass you by. And if you keep your intentions friendly, flirting can be the most straight-up and honest pastime in the world. But first you must make an honest appraisal of your needs and your attitudes. Do you ever find yourself wishing that you could start a conversation with a potential dating partner? Do you agree that there is nothing manipulative in expressing a sincere interest in a friend or acquaintance? Would it improve your life if you knew where to go, what to say, and how to fit in comfortably in any social milieu? If your answer to any of these questions is yes, your need to interact and your attitude about socializing are at odds with each other. You would be better served if you called a truce and gave yourself permission to flirt, in your own way and on your own terms.

THE SELF-CENTERED FLIRT

If your answer of choice was B, then you may be bending the ears of your prospective partners until they hurt.

Flirting is a give-and-take proposition. But conversational partners who share too much of their advice, reveal too many of their experiences, and are too vociferous about their opinions can simply be too much for anyone to take.

Here's an example. Karen was a teacher who was married to a man who controlled all the couple's finances. When her husband died suddenly at an early age, Karen found herself in dire straits. She was unable to make the complicated decisions that had been second nature to her husband—and unaccustomed to the single life. When she met Tom—a gregarious, successful businessman—at a cocktail party, she thought she had found what she needed most: a knowledgeable friend. Instead, what Tom turned out to be was a Self-Centered Flirt.

"So you're new to the singles cocktail party circuit," Tom blathered, without bothering to ascertain Karen's circumstances. "Well, I know what it's like to go from unhappily married to blissfully single. It's like getting out of prison! Yessirree, there's a lot to be said for being able to do just what you want to do without listening to a lot of static. And I'll bet a liberated, independent woman like you feels just the same way."

"Well, actually, I'm not divorced—" Karen began.

"Divorced, separated—the only difference is a settlement," Tom interrupted. "And believe me, my wife really raked it in. If she only knew how to handle a buck she'd be set for life. Like me."

"And how does a single woman get set for life in a sexist society?" snapped Karen, managing to get in a word and insult Tom with one caustic question.

Tom was oblivious. "She starts her own business, like I did," he instructed. "With the tax benefits, depreciation allowances, and a brain like mine behind you, you could be on Easy Street. It only took me five years, and I took my company from a little hole in the wall to a publicly traded corporation with three hundred employees . . . You need another drink? I'll tell you just how I did it. . . ."

Don't get me wrong. I'm not saying that all Self-Centered Flirts are insensitive louts. Many of them go on and on about their positive traits because they are insecure or desperate to be liked. Others monopolize a conversation out of nervous tension or social inexperience.

Still, if you find yourself in this category and are beginning too many sentences with the word "I," that can mean only one thing: you're turning what should be two-way conversations into self-centered soliloquies. And that invariably turns others off.

Good flirts make others feel good. You have every reason to be proud of your professional achievements and personal strengths. What you need to learn is that your virtues will shine brighter if you let others discover them on their own. Who knows ... they may even find some you never knew were there.

THE TERMINATOR FLIRT

Other flirts walk; you swagger. Other swains smile; you ogle. Some men and women are aggressive. You're the Arnold Schwarzenegger of love!

If the C answers were your choice, chances are the men and women you meet accuse you of many things— including insensitivity, sexual teasing, rampant arrogance, even harassment. In fact, with your provocative lines and libidinous leer, the only thing you probably haven't been accused of is subtlety. And that's the one virtue it's crucial for you to develop.

You might have sex on your mind, but until you learn to keep it off your lips you aren't liable to get lucky. (There aren't many mature adults who are clamoring to be treated like a one-night stand.) Give some thought to what emotions you're masking with your swagger. Many Terminator Flirts are sexual conquistadors on the outside and softies on the inside. If that description rings true for you, consider letting some of your sensitivity show. Though Terminators can be frightening, they are not bad people; they're just people with bad flirting technique.

THE PRESSURED FLIRT

An older man in my flirting seminar complained that he thought of himself as a great conversationalist who brought out his dates by asking questions they couldn't answer with a simple yes or no. Nevertheless, he couldn't find what he was looking for: an attractive, single woman who wanted to form an exclusive relationship. I asked him to role-play a conversation with a female member of the class so that I could ascertain what was going wrong.

The chat went something like this:

HE: "Boy, being married would sure beat this scene, wouldn't it?"

SHE: "I guess."

HE: "Don't you hate going out alone? Marriage is better than being single, don't you think?"

SHE: "Sometimes."

HE: "I loved being married. And I loved being around my kids. Do you like kids?"

SHE: "I do when they're someone else's."

HE: "Well, I can only speak for myself but I'm ready to settle down. Are you?"

That was all I needed to hear. He had met this woman only a few seconds earlier. Why on earth was he interrogating a virtual stranger on subjects as serious as marriage, children, and settling down? His answer was textbook Pressured Flirt. "I know what I want. I want to get married," he asserted. "So why should I waste time and energy talking to a woman who doesn't have the same goals as I do? If she wants to stay perennially single, that's fine—but she can do that on somebody else's time. If a woman feels that a wedding ring is nothing more than a fourteen-karat ball and chain, then I want to move on. And as soon as possible."

If you answered D to most of the quiz questions, you

aren't viewing flirtation as a leisurely walk down an exciting, winding road, but as a high-speed train to your ultimate destination. That's why so many of your relationships seem to get off to false starts.

Slow down! Enjoy the scenery! Flirting is not a serious, goal-oriented task. In fact, it shouldn't be a task at all. Relationships are about relating. And that means allowing each other the time to reveal yourselves, to see what—if anything—unfolds, to explore the areas where your personalities (rather than your expectations) mesh.

Don't get me wrong—I'm not advocating spending time with men and women who simply aren't your type. (Likes do attract likes, after all.) But refusing to "waste" a single moment with someone who doesn't share your future plans is a singles syndrome that will hinder you on your trip down the aisle rather than hasten it. New relationships are like new construction. First, they need a good foundation; then they get stronger as each step in the building process is completed. You wouldn't add a second story to your dream house before the walls were sturdy enough to bear it. How can you demand that a fragile new friendship stand up under the burden of your expectations?

Whether you've penciled marriage into your hidden agenda or are simply out for sex, the person who will fulfill your goals won't materialize on your schedule. Can't you just sit back and enjoy the flirting? With this book and a little patience, getting there really can be half the fun.

THE INSINCERE FLIRT

Who's the insincere flirt? She's the one showering you with compliments, batting her eyelashes in admiration, or giggling at jokes you know are flatter than a plate of milk. He's the one telling you to call EMS because you've set his heart racing in a way that can't be healthy. Sound familiar? If you tended to circle answer E, these descriptions probably do. You've used lines like these yourself—I would guess without much success.

While compliments can be great conversation-openers, most people are aware of their individual strengths and weaknesses. Hearing you expound on characteristics they feel are imperfect makes them doubt your truthfulness, your integrity, and your underlying intentions. Even if you are lucky enough to find an easily flattered companion, your sweet talk could have some very bitter effects on the outcome of the relationship. Insincere interest is very hard to sustain. Turning it on may win you points in the beginning, but turning it off will make the object of your desire grow disillusioned.

Pretending to like someone you don't means pretending to be someone you're not. Don't waste your time. There are plenty of men and women in the real world with real talents, abilities, and values for you to admire and respect. If you're having problems finding them, this book can help.

THE REJECTED FLIRT

Into each life a little rejection must fall. The trouble is that Rejected Flirts—those who answered F to most of the quiz questions—don't just expect refusals; they actually create their own.

Harry was a bright, artistic young man—a well-known illustrator and the editor of a self-published newsletter. There was little Harry couldn't do—except look on the bright side of flirting.

When Harry's friend Jack suggested that a nearby science fiction convention might be a great place to meet interesting women, Harry was pessimistic. "Good luck," he whined. "I've never met any woman who was really into science fiction. Besides, the people at those conventions are all members of the same big clique. They aren't interested in outsiders."

Not easily daunted, Jack managed to drag Harry from

his apartment. They had barely begun to browse when an attractive redhead (with an equally good-looking friend) asked Harry where she could get a quick cup of coffee. To Jack's horror, his friend pointed distractedly toward the concession.

"What are you, socially challenged?" Jack hissed, angry that his buddy had let the opportunity slip away. "We could have offered to walk them, you know!"

Harry just shrugged. "I'm telling you, Jack, women hate science fiction. If she's here, then she's here with a boyfriend. *C'est la vie.*"

Was the redhead really interested in a hit of caffeine—or was she hitting on Harry? He'll never know. And if you go to parties thinking, "There's no one here," or, "Same crowd—different day," you never will, either.

Dealing with failure and expecting failure are two very different things. If you enter each new experience with a black cloud over your head, if you reject yourself before anyone else can do it for you, it's time to give negativism the brush-off.

THE ANALYTICAL FLIRT

Is there such a thing as thinking too much? You bet there is. And my friend Mike is a perfect example.

Maybe it's because Mike is a self-described "science nerd." Maybe it's because he spends eight hours a day thinking about what data to put into his computer so that precise, predictable data will come out. But Mike simply cannot have a conversation without plotting the entire thing out in his head, from his first question to her most probable answer.

"When I see a girl I'd like to know better, the first thing I do is check her for a wedding ring," reports Mike. "Of course, sometimes married people don't wear rings, so then I have to watch awhile to see what she's up to. While

I do, I think about possible opening lines and reject the ones that don't seem appropriate."

Which conversation-starters does Mike think might be inappropriate? "I could ask about her job—but that might seem too nosy. Or I could compliment her on something she's wearing, but that might seem too personal. Sometimes I even consider walking right up and introducing myself, but I never do that. It seems too bold."

And how does Mike snap to when he's finally decided on an approach? When I asked him that, he blushed. "Well, last time I didn't do anything at all. I was so afraid of saying the wrong thing that by the time I thought of something intelligent to say, she had gotten up to dance with someone else!" If you answered G to many of the questions on the quiz, you know you don't have to be a scientist to be an Analytical Flirt. You probably also know that when it comes to flirting, he who hesitates is left behind—often for less thoughtful, concerned, and sensitive candidates.

If what you need is a ready reservoir of interesting things to say, you'll find them on page 84. If what you need is the kind of pep talk that will make you stop thinking and start flirting, you'll find that on page 20.

In fact, no matter what kind of flirt you are, this book is sure to make you a more attractive, successful one. Based on the same effective techniques that have worked for thousands of my workshop graduates, drawn from more than ten years of research and study, this invaluable guide to making it in today's singles market is a sourcebook of secrets you can use to attract anyone you want, anywhere you are, anytime you choose.

And to you skeptics still doubtful that you can go from bashful to belle of the ball, think about this: no matter how shy you may be, no matter how many romances you've terminated with your Terminator style, flirting becomes you. That's because a flirt is something none of us has to *try* to become.

BABY, WE WERE BORN TO FLIRT

Admit it. You've used that winsome smile of yours to cajole others out of innumerable intimate dinners, countless impromptu drinks, and dozens of spontaneous matinees. And with those twinkling eyes, you've brought otherwise staid businesspeople and somber adults to their knees—and then repaid them for their effort by drooling on their shoes.

As babies, we were all natural, exuberant flirts. And because we didn't have language to rely on, we won over the world with our gummy grins, our innocent appeal, and our fun-loving sense of adventure. Without ever saying a word, we captivated everyone within reach of our open arms. And without ever asking, or pressuring, or wheedling, we were fed, entertained, and nurtured in every conceivable way.

After you've outgrown the baby fat, the fine art of flirting still works in precisely that way. Smile and the world smiles with you. Approach the people you meet with an open manner and you will not only be attracted to others, but others will be attracted to you.

Of course, for many of us, that's easier said than done. Once we stop charting our growth with notches on the doorjamb and start measuring up to life in the real world, the guileless skills we learned as babies fall by the wayside. By the time we're adolescents, our emotions aren't something we share—they're something we mask. By the time we hit college, we are consciously stifling our natural flirtatiousness. As adults, we are so far removed from what began as natural behavior that the very idea of flirting seems somehow false, manipulative, or insincere. But is it insincere to admit that you are looking for companionship and to pursue it? I don't think so. And is it deceitful to learn to socialize effectively, to sharpen your communication skills, to use body language to send a positive, confident message? If you thought so, you wouldn't be holding this book in your hands.

This guide isn't about turning you into something you aren't. It's about putting you in touch with the natural flirt you already are. As Dale Carnegie once said, "If you go fishing, you may like strawberries but you put a worm at the end of the hook 'cause the fish likes worms." You had that wisdom in your pocket before you were a year old. Now's the perfect time to dust it off and put it into practice.

CONVERSATION: THE SEXUALITY OF THE '90S

Funny thing about revolutions: they never end. And so it goes with the sexual revolution. In the 1960s, when love and flowers were free, we answered the call of freedom by jumping into bed with every Tom, Dick, or Moonstar we found appealing. The freewheeling '70s brought more of the same—and ushered in the idea of disco dance as foreplay. But in the age of HIV and so many other sexually transmitted diseases, the green light turned red. Conversation became the accepted form of sexuality. Suddenly we needed to get to know our partners, their habits, and their history. And flirting—or acting amorously without serious intent—came back into vogue as the first step in establishing communication.

Of course, revolutions don't happen without casualties. Many of us still feel more comfortable grappling with virtual strangers than with social change. Others just feel left behind. As one man in my seminar put it, "First the rules changed. Then the style of play changed. Now dating is a whole new ballgame and I'm sitting on the bench!"

No doubt about it, the bench is the hardest seat in the house. But if you're observant, that chair you're warming can give you a front-and-center view of how flirting functions as today's number-one attraction. Just claim a spot in your favorite hangout and watch awhile. Who are the savvy singles who seem to "have it"? One look will tell you that they weren't first in line when God passed out the beauty. And most of the time, their accessories don't include cars like Mario Andretti's. In fact, the most successful flirts around are men and women just like you who have learned to put others at ease with a smile, or to present what may be some rather ordinary characteristics in a truly unique way. And if that news knocks you off your seat, all the better! As the 2,500 flirts who have passed through my seminar will tell you, you can't put your best foot forward when you're sitting on the bench. And the time to take the first positive strides into the wonderful world of flirting is *now*.

WHAT FLIRTING CAN DO FOR YOU

Flirtation is a subtle, playful skill that works its magic in any social milieu. It will fill your life with interesting, attractive people, enlarge your social circle, and make you more appealing to the special men and women you've always wanted to meet but never dared approach.

Of course, flirting is not an asbestos suit. It will not insulate you against rejection. But it will enable you to accept yourself for who you are, enhance your awareness of others' needs, and give you all the people skills you need to reduce rejection to a minimum.

Finally, flirting will certainly make business a more satisfying place to be! Based on hundreds of practical, proven techniques, drawn from the real-world experiences of real-life flirts, my surefire strategies will help you to develop a vital network of friendly contacts, charm your way into the job of your dreams, and enable you to attract anyone, anytime, anyplace ... whether you're in the office or in the great outdoors.

SECRETS OF THE MASTER FLIRT

Developing the ultimate flirting style sounds daunting, I know. But reduce the secrets of the Master Flirt to their most elemental form and they come down to this: flirting is the fine art of relating to others and allowing others to relate to you.

The flirt within you cannot be contrived because it cannot be created. This book is about rediscovering yourself as the playful, adventurous person you already are and, in the process, becoming the best flirt you can be.

Do you have what it takes to be a Master Flirt? I know you do. There are only two requirements: Relax! Enjoy!

TIPS FROM A MASTER FLIRT

Remember:

- An "I Don't Flirt" Flirt is an "I Don't Get" Flirt. Give yourself a break! Give yourself permission to relate.
- Nothing terminates encounters faster than a Terminator approach. Give others time to get to know you.
- Your job, car, or inflated ego is not an aphrodisiac. Showing as much interest in your partner's achievements as you do in your own is the ultimate turn-on.
- Negative thinking never leads to positive action. Change your mind and you'll change your luck.
- People can spot an insincere compliment from a mile away—that's why false flatterers get nowhere with the opposite sex.
- Flirting should be spontaneous. Live the moment! Don't plan too much!
- Conversations you have in your head tend to stay there. If you see someone you're interested in, act!
- Flirting isn't about fantasy. It is a real skill that will make you successful in the real world.
- You were born to flirt! To make the most of your natural inclinations, read on!

2

MAKING YOUR OWN LUCK

"My friend Sally gets more good men than the Army. She always seems to be at the right place at the right time."

—ANNE, age 22

"Lucky in cards, unlucky in love ... and I play a mean game of poker."

—RON, age 45

You know them. Men who wear the grubbiest sweats and drive jalopies—yet are always adding to the waiting list of lovely, vivacious women who want to ride in the passenger seat. We all know them. Women who run their stockings, break a heel, and somehow always manage to fall into the arms of the men of our dreams. We don't hate them because they're beautiful. Often they're not. What we resent them for is the uncanny sense of direction that always seems to lead them straight to the right place at exactly the right time. They aren't insufferable people. They're just insufferably lucky.

Or are they? Read this story, then judge for yourself. At a conference for sexologists in Toronto, I got the flirting opportunity of a lifetime. I was walking through the lobby of my hotel, wearing my most attractive emerald-green dress and a badge that read, "Susan G. Rabin, M.A.— Society for the Scientific Study of Sex," when a good-looking middle-aged gentleman approached me.

"Is that for real?" he asked with a twinkle in his eye and a charming smile.

"Yes, it is," I answered, "though my mother never seems to believe me when I tell her what we actually accomplish at these conferences."

"I can understand why," the man said, laughing. "In our own way, I think we all study sex our entire lives. And in the end, we still don't seem to know much more than when we began."

"I agree," I said, checking my watch. "But I'm here to learn all I can, and right now I'm off to hear a talk on the history of the sexual revolution—"

"I hope it's not over yet—the revolution, that is," the man teased.

Here I was, flirting's biggest proponent. And here it was, a perfect opportunity to get to know a dashing, intelligent stranger. Did I laugh at his joke? No. Did I give him my card so that we could get together at a more convenient time? No. What did I do? I checked my watch again so that I could become even more preoccupied with the possibility of missing that day's opening remarks. Focused more on where I was going than on what I was doing, I smiled— then abruptly walked away.

As my Canadian friend and I had too briefly discussed, dating, relating, and mating aren't just encounters we pursue, they are social sciences we study. As a therapist, a teacher, and a student, I have explored the various mixes that make up sexual chemistry. But that day in Toronto I learned a lesson in a hotel lobby that couldn't have been taught to me in any seminar. I learned that fortune in the social sphere isn't something you're blessed or cursed with. On that day, with that man, I had made my own luck. And I vowed that from then on, I would pay attention to the kind of destiny I was creating for myself. I would only make luck of a more positive kind.

If you've been thinking that only fortuitous flirts get all the breaks, think again! Are your priorities out of order? Have you been wasting your time on inappropriate people? Then you're jinxing your prospects—and wasting your time. Are you missing opportunities? Do you put the kibosh on impromptu conversations? Then you're shutting serendipity out of your life.

The six savvy guidelines in this chapter changed my success with the opposite sex—and they can change yours, too. Use them like a roadmap and you'll always chart a course to the right place at the right time.

#1: GET OUT OF THE HOUSE.

Couch potatoes, wake up! Cozying up in front of the TV may be a great way to detox after a long day at work, but if you're spending night after night in front of the boob tube the only person you're likely to meet is the TV repairman. And that's only if you're lucky enough to lose your reception.

We all need time to chill out, be alone, regroup. But unless you break your self-imposed exile and get out where the action is, you may be hibernating alone for a very long time.

Make sure your door opens both ways. Choose three nights out of the week, mark them as unbreakable dates on your calendar, and when the time comes, hit the streets.

Accept no last-minute excuses from yourself, either. We've all had nights when we were dragged from our lairs by friends who wouldn't take no for an answer—and we ended up having a ball. So give yourself a pep talk. Light a fire under your La-Z-Boy. Pretend your forays are a second job if you have to. But get out of your doldrums!

One more thing: we are as isolated in our cars as we are in our homes. Walking to the bank, the drugstore, or the local hangout gives you a chance to make friends with your neighbors—and good neighbors can make for good flirting.

#2: TO MEET INTERESTING PEOPLE, GO TO INTERESTING PLACES.

If you're anything like the singles who attend my seminars, I know just what you're thinking. "I've been everywhere between here and Timbuktu and I still haven't met anyone." I even had one ravishingly handsome young man shrug off the possibility that he'd been looking for love in all the wrong places. When I suggested that he check out my list of suggested places to meet and flirt (you'll find it on page 146), he brushed me off with a curt "Been there. Done that."

Okay. So maybe you've done the local bar/dance/theater circuit to death. Maybe you've logged in enough time at the singles health club to become the next Mr. or Ms. Celibate Olympia. Or maybe you've been out and about so long that even the sight of a poppit bead brings about instantaneous Club Med déjà vu. If you aren't making the rounds with an open mind, if you aren't approaching each new experience with an adventurous spirit, you haven't been anywhere!

So where are all these fascinating destinations? And why are all the intriguing people of the world hiding there? It should be obvious. The most interesting places to go are those places that are interesting to you. Who else would you expect to find in friendly territory but people who share your interests, who add to your knowledge ... who can, in short, be friends?

Janet, a woman I met in my seminar, is a case in point. At the time she was learning to flirt, she had just completed a course in homeopathy. Although she wasn't convinced that natural, herbal medicines could cure the allergies that had plagued her for years, she found the holistic approach—and the people who shared her "otherworldly pursuits"—fascinating.

For a while, she felt alone in her interest. Her friends were disdainful of New Age ideology. Her parents thought she had gone off the deep end without a life preserver. But Janet was not easily deterred. When she heard that a Whole Life Expo was in full swing at a local hotel, she broke her longtime habit of finding a friend to accompany her and drove in from the suburbs alone. Before she knew it, Janet was too busy collecting leaflets and browsing through books on natural remedies to care whether anyone had come with her. And when her eye caught a demonstration of a unique machine that both baked bread and made yogurt, she blended right in to the circle of spectators.

"Isn't it amazing," she blurted out to the man next to her. "This machine is able to bake bread and produce yogurt—all with the press of a button! I think I could make use of that."

"I bought this machine last year and I love it," answered the man. "I don't use it to make yogurt, though. Dannon does it better."

Now Janet turned to take a better look at this stranger. He was a ruggedly attractive blond with a well-trimmed beard. Was it his appearance or his gentle sense of humor that had captivated her? She was dying to find out. "Do you like yogurt?" she asked.

"Frozen, stir-up, or blended, it's my lunch, day in, day

out," the man replied. "In fact, my stomach is grumbling for some right now."

"They're giving away samples at the booth over there," Janet prompted. "Active cultures only."

The man smiled. "Then what are we waiting for?" He whisked Janet across the aisle and led her into the crowd.

What are you waiting for? Whether you are turned on by a bicycle trip through New York's Little Italy, a motor tour through the Smoky Mountains, a lecture at the Museum of Natural History, a square-dance club, a community auction, or a gourmet cooking class, there are hundreds of vital, single people in your community who share your interests. So why haven't you met any of them in the local tavern? Because these people are doers! They're too busy enrolling, participating, and enjoying to sit there watching the ice melt in a bar glass.

Suppose you're thinking that the time has come to melt some ice of your own. Where do you begin? First, take pen in hand and make a list of the hobbies, talents, and interests you'd most like to develop. Start with activities you already pursue on your own, such as photography or listening to music, then let your imagination run wild. If you're landlocked in Sante Fe but have yearned to try windsurfing, write that down. If you've always liked to sing but your ex-girlfriend said you croaked like a frog, underline that entry in red. (It'll make you feel better about giving her the old heave-ho.)

Now, with your list in hand, begin to think of ways you can pursue your heart's desire and flirt at the same time. Hooked on books? Check the college paper to see whether there's a visiting author who'll be speaking, or join a contemporary fiction discussion group at the local library. Like to hike? Scour the singles papers for regional hiking clubs, ask your travel agent for information on fly/hike packages, or, if you're daring, take a class in skydiving. If you still aren't sure where to go, search the yellow pages, newspapers, or community bulletin board for possible outlets. You'll find hundreds of clubs or organizations that can turn your personal interests into group activities. My yellow pages even list a mushroom-pickers' association! How's that for personalized service?

Getting in touch with the subjects and activities that stimulate you gives you insight into the kind of partner who will make your life complete. Pursuing those interests may even put you within striking range of that very special person.

And if the love of your life doesn't two-step into your arms at the country-Western dancing class you've joined, so what? Once you've learned to dance (or cook, or brew your own beer), finding appreciative partners is the easy part. And the experience isn't a waste of your energy, because you've had an enjoyable evening and don't feel depressed, as singles often say they do when they go out to meet, sit at a bar all evening, and connect with no one. Singles bars often exaggerate the feeling of being lonely in a crowd, and you can go home feeling like a grounded barfly.

#3: SAVE TIME AND ENERGY.

Jackie was a true country-music devotee. Her radio dial was glued to the local "twang and twirl" station. Yet she was convinced that the man of her dreams would be much more sophisticated and highbrow than she. Uncomfortable as she was in formal attire, and as unknowledgeable as she was about the differences between Bach and Beethoven, Jackie joined a classical-music-lovers' group in her area, certain that it was the key to finding a man she could love.

The group was stuffy and inbred, but Jackie swept in like a breath of fresh air. With her unusual good looks and quiet style, she took the young men in the club by storm. By the end of the first meeting, she had made a concert date with Brad, a Mozart aficionado.

Unfortunately, Jackie's unconscious image of the man of her dreams didn't do much to keep her conscious during the concert. When Brad turned to ask her whether she was enjoying herself, he found her sound asleep. Worst of all, she wasn't very stimulating after the performance, either. She simply wasn't interested in Brad's opinions about the maestro's avant-garde interpretation. And Brad could fit everything she had to offer into the end of a piccolo.

Needless to say, Jackie couldn't face Brad or the other members of the club again. But she did eventually face up to the truth of the matter: when you try to be someone you aren't, you attract people who aren't right for you. And that is always a waste of time, money, and energy.

#4: MAKE ANYPLACE WORK FOR YOU.

I love ski-lift lines. They're the only place in the world where you can yell, "Single!" and not be looked at like the Vamp of Aspen. Chairlifts are also the only place where you can hold an attractive prospect legally captive for fifteen uninterrupted minutes while you charm him or her into meeting you for an après-ski hot toddy.

Unfortunately, you can't shout your availability everywhere you go. (That is definitely not a strategy that wins hearts in the grocery line!) But you can make yourself known without making a scene. All it takes is the willingness to consider anyplace a meeting place, the ingenuity to use virtually anything as conversational kindling, and the openness to accept everybody as a potential friend. How do I know this approach will work for you? It worked for a gentleman who nearly outflirted me!

I couldn't help noticing the nice-looking man who boarded the crosstown bus with me one sunny afternoon. For one thing, he ushered me into the line in front of him, which let me know he had good manners. For another, he had a smile that was as bright as the day—and he wasn't stingy when it came to sharing it. We proceeded to the back of the empty bus and took seats facing each other.

That he was very pleasant to look at, I already knew. What he was about to tell me was that the feeling was mutual. As soon as he sat down, we engaged each other in a playful dialogue with our eyes. First we caught each other's glance, then promptly looked away. We repeated this action three times until I looked up at the advertisement above his head, curious to see whether his eyes would still be focused on me when I looked back at him. They were. Again I looked up and read the curious ad in silence ("Chamomile tea is good for the nerves; peppermint for the stomach"), looked down, our eyes met, and I looked away. We were playing Lingering Looks and Peek-a-Boo Glances. The game went on for a full ten minutes—until we got off the bus together.

It didn't take long before I began to get the distinct feeling that he was shadowing me. I crossed the street; so did he. I stopped in a small grocery store; so did he. When I got in line to pay for my purchase, he was right behind me. I turned sharply to confront him—but I was beaten to the punch. "I'm not following you, honestly," he said with a smile.

His open, kindly manner reassured me. But he seemed intent on proving that his intentions were aboveboard. He broke my gaze, giving me time to consider his explanation. Then he exchanged greetings with the man behind the counter.

"Do you know this man?" I asked the grocer.

"Oh, yes," he replied. "Very well."

"She thought I was following her," my gentlemanly acquaintance explained.

"If you were, I don't blame you," the grocer said. "She's very pretty."

With that, I relaxed totally. And my new friend proceeded to fill me on his plans for the day—which definitely did not include tailing me. The store I had happened into was his neighborhood market. He was there to pick up some ice cream to snack on while watching the afternoon football game. His motives were all-American.

When I finally went on my way, my new acquaintance was with me. He had gallantly asked to escort me to my destination: a lecture in a nearby building. As it turned out, it was the first of many walks, countless talks, and the beginning of a terrific three-year romance.

As I told you in the introduction to this book, the graduates of my seminars have turned every possible locale—including salad bars, ski lodges, motorcycle races, kite-flying contests, and post offices—into fertile flirting ground. Of course, sometimes it takes a little bit of planning to strategize a "chance" encounter with an attractive stranger. But a small investment in effort and thought can pay off big-time, as it did for Marty, a student I know.

At 8:30 every morning, Marty staked out a spot for himself at the subway station. There he waited, photography equipment in tow, for the train that would take him to his television production course at New York University. City subways are not prompt. Weighted down as he was with cameras, lenses, and books, Marty's wait might have seemed interminable had he not noticed the knockout smile of a female fellow rider.

All Marty knew about his mass transit mystery woman was this: she, too, caught the train every weekday morning at 8:30. The two girlfriends who kept her company on the platform called her Elissa. And she had the kind of smile that Marty desperately wanted to capture with his camera.

But how? This was a big-city subway station. The people who waited there had big-city suspicions. Marty didn't want to come off as a pervert. So day after day, he smiled politely in her direction—and she smiled back. Morning after morning, he vowed that he would speak to her—then kicked himself for not having summoned the courage. Finally, Marty did what any self-respecting paparazzo would do: he photographed her from behind a distant newsstand using a wide-angle lens.

The developed photo did for Marty what hair did for Samson. The next time he encountered the woman, he marched right up, introduced himself, and blurted out the details of his undercover work. "I'm studying photography and I hope you won't think I'm fresh, but we had a project on smiles and I loved yours, so I took the liberty of photographing you without your permission."

Marty could see that Elissa was struggling to regain her composure. The smile he had so admired was nowhere in sight. Nervous now, he babbled on. "I'm sorry if this seems a little brazen. But it's a prize-winning photograph and I'd love to show it to you. Would it be possible to meet here tomorrow morning, say, half an hour earlier than usual? Or at the coffee shop on the street corner? I could even make up an extra print for your boyfriend."

It seemed to take Elissa forever to respond. "I suppose I could do that," she answered finally, not wanting to give Marty too much encouragement. "I would like to see the picture." Just then, the train rattled into the station. "By the way," Elissa added, "I don't have a boyfriend to show it to."

The subway doors closed—but a whole new chapter opened up for Elissa and Marty. Of course, you may call Marty's planned "Why-don't-you-come-out-and-see-my-prints-sometime" technique manipulation. I call it smart. Successful flirting takes forethought and attention. To me (and Marty!), studying up on the object of your flirtation before making an approach is no more manipulative than reading up on a company before sending a résumé. And that's the way I feel about the next rule, as well ...

#5: HAVE A FLIRTING PROP.

If this were a geometry class, this rule would be a corollary to guideline #2. Interesting people do go to interesting places ... but really fascinating flirts carry evidence of their hobbies, pastimes, and talents around with them. Whether you're into dogs, vintage clothing, books, outrageous ties, Mickey Mouse watches, or riveted leather wristbands, the things you wear and essentials you carry aren't just objets d'art—they're bits and pieces of your unique personality. Put them on display and they make the world a more stimulating place for all of us. Wear them with pride and they can make you a virtually irresistible flirt.

What makes a flirting prop work? First, it catches the eye. Second, it functions as a decoy to take the focus off the flirtation. My own flirting prop—a large, totally camp tortoiseshell ring with a huge glass stone—is a prime example. Big enough to attract more than its share of comments, it has gotten me interrogated ("Is that real?"), dated ("Is that a Captain Marvel ring from the fifties?"), warned ("You really shouldn't wear diamonds in the subway these days!") and made me the center of many good-natured jokes ("I see you carry your own flashlight!"). It has also enabled countless shy souls to do what they otherwise could not: express an interest in me by expressing an interest in my flirting prop.

Your antique hat, astrology book, or college beer mug may not seem like much, but knickknacks like these give interested parties something other than you to comment on. And that helps less secure flirts save face while getting to know you a little better. At least, that's the way it worked for one natural flirt who dazzled my seminar with a flirting prop no one could overlook.

Randy made his first appearance in my workshop wearing canary-yellow suspenders against a light-yellow shirt. The moment I began conversing with him it was clear that his ensemble didn't just make a fashion statement. It was a conversation-starter.

"They say that red is a power color, but I love that yellow," I said enthusiastically.

"Thanks. I picked these up at a flea market," Randy answered.

"Are they antique?"

Now Randy's rap really took off. "No, but the man who sold them to me certainly was," he said with a laugh. "I asked the guy what they were doing among his old books and hats. He told me he bought them from a street vendor years ago and wore them ever since—until his wife put an end to it. She bought him a red and green pair for Christmas but wouldn't give them to him unless he promised to ditch the yellow ones. So he put them up for sale."

"You mean this was the only pair of suspenders he sold?"

Randy nodded. "That's right. And now that I've been wearing them awhile, I know exactly why his wife wanted him to get rid of them. As soon as I put them on, some lovely lady comments. . . ."

And as soon as some lovely lady comments, Randy is off and running with the story of the antique man and his nagging mate. His fortunate find at the flea market not only netted him some very fine suspenders to show off, it gave him a forum through which he could display his wit, intelligence, and charm.

Of course, some of us don't wear showy embellishments well. My friend Justine wouldn't be caught dead in biking pants or a bubble necklace. But she has hooked many men with the books she carries.

Justine's favorite books had titles like *Victoria's Secret Awakening* and *Dawn of Desire*. For her, these romantic epics made great bedtime reading. But Justine was a clever bookworm. She knew men seldom read romance novels. She also knew that gothic fiction commonly had titles with sexual overtones—and she didn't want erotic nuances clouding her meetings with available men. Since the man she was looking for was someone who could be interested in her, not her sexual fantasies, she left the romances on the nighttable. What she picked up instead was a copy of *How to Buy and Sell Country Property*.

Now, Justine *did* have a genuine interest in owning a country home. (It may have been a financially impossible dream, but it was her dream nonetheless.) And she was smart enough to have begun reading the book before debuting it in public. If a man asked questions, Justine would have the answers. And sure enough, as soon as she propped the book up at a local beach, a man began to look in her direction. Before she could say "tax shelter," he was at her side, explaining that he had found a prime piece of real estate in the Berkshires—and asking for pointers on how to assess its value in a volatile market.

Barry Farber, the radio personality and financial consultant, also uses books as flirting aids—and with a very specific goal in mind. "I like tall, Nordic blonds," he told me, "and I happen to speak seven languages." The man is not just a successful broadcaster—he's a veritable United Nations of Flirtdom! But he never leaves home without his Swedish, Danish, Norwegian, and German language guides. That way, when he sees a Scandinavian or German woman, he can pull out the appropriate volume and stammer a greeting in her native tongue. Of course, this wily, inventive flirt is fluent enough to begin a conversation without a phrasebook. But Barry Farber knows that vulnerability is appealing. And he is as unapologetic about showing some as he is about his flirting props.

What kinds of books top the best-seller list for high-minded flirts? Those with titles like *Success* or *How to Swim with the Sharks* will always attract the attention of the business crowd. Guidebooks are effective props even if you're in your native land. (Yes, you can ask directions even if you know exactly where you're going!) But if you really want to hold someone's attention, *try the book you're holding now*. It not only sends the message that you're interested in improving your social skills, it lets the world know that you're available. It's hard to imagine a more effective flirting prop than that.

As for ineffective flirting props . . . here's a cautionary note. A fellow in my workshop came in sporting a button on his jacket that read, "Sexy Man—Step Up and Inquire Within." It pushed the buttons of every woman in the room. Sexual advertising is a real turn-off. Allowing provocative T-shirts or buttons to speak for you broadcasts an adolescent mentality, a juvenile sense of humor, and an air of sexual desperation. In short, they aren't props at all— they are crutches for an injured ego.

Flirting props should be the modern-day equivalent of the dropped hanky or the fluttering fan. Choose yours with care, display it playfully, and while you're waiting for a response, read the next guideline. You'll need it!

#6: BE OPEN TO ADVANCES.

Sometimes we singles get so hung up on how, when, and where to flirt with others, we overlook the possibility that others may be trying desperately to flirt with us. The only thing I've found that's more fun than flirting is flirting back. So why not cut those interested parties some slack?

First, separate from your old friends so that new friends can approach you. Gathering a congenial mob to escort you to a party ensures that there will be someone there you can talk to, but stick with the same old crowd and you'll remain a mystery to attractive strangers who'd like to get to know you better.

Women, take my advice: don't travel in herds. Over the years, I've listened to hundreds of men discuss "the one that got away." Nine out of ten times, she was the one they couldn't get away from her buddies. If you simply can't socialize comfortably alone, arrange to separate from your friends for a half hour or so to mingle with party guests you don't know, or relax by the bar. That will give anyone who's interested a chance to stroll over without feeling like a third wheel, or ask you to dance without worrying about whether your friend will be insulted.

If you're still concerned about being cornered by a man you don't care for, work out a signal system that will enable your friends to come to your rescue. A clever flirt I know has informed her comrades that if she catches their glance, then touches her necklace, that means she has definitely happened into friendly territory. They should leave her alone. If, on the other hand, her friends see her pulling on her earring, they know she needs an ally and an exit. They come to her aid at once.

As for you men—think twice about those impenetrable he-man huddles in the corner of the room or at the bar. Get-togethers are for just that. So what if it's Monday night and you're suffering from football deprivation? You can get the latest scores from the sports hotline, but you won't get female companionship without making an effort to socialize.

By the way, some of the most successful flirts I know have made their own luck by rubbing elbows with everyone who comes their way—not just the handpicked few they find especially compelling. If becoming a Universal Flirt seems like a waste of time to you, consider this: acquaintances can become friends—and friends have other, attractive connections they can introduce you to. So what if you and your latest party conquest lack sexual chemistry? Networking and flirting are wildly compatible! Friend-of-a-friend contacts often bring about new jobs, new romance, or (watch out!) even marriage. After all, how many married people look adoringly at their lifetime mate and tell you they weren't even attracted to or interested in this person when they first met? So don't limit yourself. Stay open to the advances of others. You never know who may be able to open some important doors.

BE PREPARED

The simple strategies I've outlined in this chapter don't require a great deal of time, a major cash outlay, or even concerted effort. But if you've been putting them into practice, you are probably feeling luckier already!

Be prepared. Now's the time to plan for even greater flirting success. If you have a business card, start carrying it with you wherever you go. Sharing a conversation is fun—but sharing your home phone number with every attractive stranger you meet *isn't* wise, especially for women. If you are a man, think about having a personal card printed up. You can hand them out, like compliments, to a special few—or send one, accompanied by a drink or a single rose, to a woman's restaurant table for a particularly romantic touch.

Giving your private number lets a woman know that you have selected her to become a part of your personal life. It also reassures her that "all the good ones"—notably you—really *aren't* taken.

One more thing: if you've already gotten lucky and you're wondering where to go with that interesting person you've just met, then put this in your database. Meeting for coffee (or anything nonalcoholic) is much safer than getting together for drinks. You won't say what you don't mean, and you won't do what you'll wish you hadn't. And if dinner seems too intimate, try lunch. Daytime dates are friendly, unassuming. You can meet and eat without worrying about a good-night kiss. Best of all, midday meals are fast. If the date goes well, you'll part as interesting mysteries to each other. If the date goes badly, you can beat a hasty retreat without looking rude. Just pick up the check as soon as it hits the table, say thanks, and part cordially. On your way out, check your watch. You may even have a few minutes left over to try your flirting skills on someone else!

HOW TO MAKE YOUR OWN LUCK

Remember:

- ❤ Get out of the house! Watching *Love Connection* and actually making one aren't compatible.
- ❤ Develop a varied list of hobbies and pastimes. Be a Renaissance Flirt.
- ❤ To get into the swing of things in your community, get out of your car. It's a rolling isolation chamber.
- ❤ Have a flirting prop. Anything that suggests your uniqueness without being threatening will do.
- ❤ Don't just pursue flirtation—pursue your natural talents and interests.
- ❤ Chance encounters sometimes need a little strategy to help them along. If a meeting isn't happening, make it happen.
- ❤ Anyplace can be a meeting place. Make where you are work for you.
- ❤ Be open and approachable—even if you're approached by people who are not your type.
- ❤ Wedding bells will never break up that old gang of yours as long as you are content to be one of the crowd. Don't travel in herds.
- ❤ Take the initiative: other people are shy, too!

3

FLIRTING 101—
THE BASICS

There's language in her eye, her cheek, her lip,
Nay, her foot speaks; her wanton spirits look out
At every joint and motive of her body.
                                        —WILLIAM SHAKESPEARE

"I saw this incredible woman waiting to cross the street. And
I know she saw me. Her hair was red and wild. Her lips
were red and wild. And she had the kind of body that
screamed, 'Spend a day with me and you'll die happy.' Un-
fortunately, the whole thing caught me so off guard, I stared
down into the gutter. Everything about her said, 'Sex.' Every-
thing about me said, 'Dweeb.'"   —ROBERT, age 24

What I love most about a story like Robert's is that everyone can relate to it. Who hasn't felt so mesmerized by

someone else's beauty, knowledge, or spine-tingling presence? I know I have. And who hasn't—at least once—felt
as confident, appealing, and sexually charged as Robert's
mystery woman? We all have. What's more, we all *can* feel
like that a lot more often than we think.

Flirting—the fine art of noticing and being noticed by
others—doesn't take extraordinary looks, immense wealth,
outstanding brains, noteworthy talent, or a body that
screams anything at all. What it takes is awareness. No
matter what kind of package or mood you're in, if you are
aware of the feelings and desires of others you can bring
out the interesting, vital side of everyone you meet. And
that will make you a more interesting, vital person to others.

Is it really that simple? Yes! In my research and in my
workshops, I've come across thousands of self-described
plain Janes and Joes who have had enormous success
meeting anyone they want, anytime they choose, anywhere
they are. Some of them really weren't plain at all, but
thought they were. Others were plain, but thought they
weren't. But all of them made the most of what they had:
eyes that were full of life, ready smiles, and the uncanny
ability to draw people in, then bring out the best in them.

In this chapter you'll learn the three basic skills that
will put you in the enviable position of being able to focus
on what you want, flirt with confidence, and walk away a
winner in the singles game. These fundamentals, which I
call the Big Three, are eye contact, smile savvy, and body
language—and their effect on your life can be enormous
and immediate. So if you haven't already, make room in
your date book! These invaluable skills are the bare essentials, but they are all you need to get out there, get noticed,
and start flirting.

Where to begin? Let's take it from the top.

THE EYES HAVE IT

If Cleopatra were alive today, she would be the potent, provocative woman Robert encountered on the street corner. Okay, so Cleopatra's flirting took a venomous turn. And maybe you're reading this book just so that you can avoid another date with a snake. But Cleopatra understood and used the power in her eyes. She enhanced them with secret kohl mixtures prepared by her most trusted servants. And she made sure that no lover ever caught sight of her until her eyes were adorned to reflect her political strength and sexual stamina.

In truth, Cleo could have saved a few shekels on live-in makeup artists. Naturally enhanced by the brows, surrounded by the most sensitive and pliant skin on the body, even the plainest eyes are limitlessly expressive features. Every minute of every day, they work like barometers, telegraphing our stormiest moods, communicating our warmest feelings, and revealing whether conflicting pressures are at work inside us.

For a glimpse at the eyes' power to attract and repel, all you have to do is conjure up an image of a face, then read the following descriptive phrases: an icy stare; a furtive glance; a deadly glare; bedroom eyes; a lingering gaze; a mocking look. Get the picture? The emotions that slip through the windows of the soul are so compelling that simply calling them to mind evokes a palpable response in us. It isn't hard to see, then, how real people must react when confronted with our looks, gazes, and glares.

Making eye contact is a twofold process. First you must understand how your eye movements affect others; then you can practice using your eyes to transmit your interest (or lack of interest) in someone in particular. Of course, in flirting, the messages you want to send are *always* positive. Laughing eyes encourage companionship. "Steely gazes" alienate and few have the interest or patience to break through. So how can you be sure you're transmitting a fascinating come-hither look instead of a withering glare? By using your eyes with admiration and respect rather than aggression.

THE FLIRTING TRIANGLE

"It happened at one of those nightclubs where a bouncer decides whether you look good enough to get in," Paul reported after a long, hard weekend. "I saw this knockout of a girl standing in line so I caught her eye and smiled. She sort of smiled back, then looked away. After a while, I glanced in her direction again. This time she whispered something to her friends. They looked over, but she looked away again. To me, it seemed like she was doing some kind of a peekaboo thing, so the next time she peeked at me, I stared her straight in the eye. Next thing I know, the bouncer's in my face. He says, 'Listen weirdo, if you don't stop staring at this lady, I'll bounce you out of here. Okay?' "

While making eye contact is necessary if you want to catch someone's attention, the idea is not to catch flak while you're at it!

The way you look at others has a great deal to do with the way they look back at you. Although some men continue to use it, a wink is a sexually suggestive eye gesture that repels many women. Raised eyebrows (you know— that explicit "woo-woo" look) are another no-no. And staring is definitely taboo. Pinning a person down with an unbreakable gaze is the equivalent of spearing him or her on a skewer. Threatened and uneasy, our targets have no alternative but to run. As I explained it to Paul, staring is considered a direct threat in the animal kingdom. It is a look that large carnivores use to mesmerize their prey before an attack. And good flirts never attack!

"Flirt" is a friendly verb. That's why it's crucial that every gesture, movement, and glance associated with flirting be light, gregarious, and unintimidating. The challenge is how to make your interest known without coming off as too obvious, too aggressive, or downright desperate.

When it comes to taking the hard focus off eye contact, nothing beats this simple technique. Think of the face as a triangle with its widest points at the corners of the forehead, tapering down to the tip of the chin. Now imagine that you are an artist and that the flirting triangle—the area from hairline to jawline—is your canvas. Move your eyes over it as lightly, playfully, and respectfully as you would your brush.

Instead of staring directly into your partner's eyes, let your glance wander from his brow to his temples; from her earlobe to her chin. Now and then, allow your eyes to meet briefly, then continue your exploration, barely touching each part of the face with a gaze that is always lighter than air.

As Paul's story shows us, limiting your eye contact strictly to a partner's eye area can be off-putting—or even hazardous to your health. Using the flirting triangle broadens your target, making it almost impossible to stare, gawk, or threaten.

So how can you tell whether you're using the triangle to best advantage? Easy! The flirting triangle functions as a stare-diffuser. While this technique should enable you to establish your presence with others, its effect should be subtle enough to use on anybody. If you are as comfortable exploring your boss's flirting triangle as you are the face of an intriguing stranger, then you can be sure that you are using your eyes in a compelling way rather than an unnerving one.

THE BASIC EYE MOVEMENTS

"Glance, gaze ... what's the difference? The women I know would be happy just to find a guy who can look them in the eye."
                                        —MICHELLE, age 33

Michelle enjoyed playing the part of the resident cynic in my seminar group, but eventually even she had to admit that there is a big difference among a glance, a gaze, and a gawk—particularly if you happen to be on the receiving end of those very distinctive looks.

Body language experts tell us that of all the parts of the human body used to transmit information (and *every* part of the body transmits information constantly), only the eyes can telegraph our emotions with nuance and depth. From the lingering, seductive gaze that says, "I'd really like to get to know you," to the brief, teasing glances that speak of playful interest, our eye gestures reveal volumes about our secret desires and intentions.

But if our eye movements are as complex as our emotions, doesn't that make them difficult to read? You bet. Many singles, like Michelle, equate straight-on eye contact with straight-up virtues like honesty, loyalty, and guilelessness. But prolonged looks or outright gawks aren't just confrontational, they're downright insulting. Gaping at people the way we do a television set or inspecting them as if they were paintings in a gallery lets them know that we see them as objects rather than as people—and nobody is likely to be swept off her feet by a misguided flirt who treats other human beings as if they were his personal home entertainment center.

Although we don't usually think of them as such, eye movements are gestures that can either beckon others closer or wave them away. If you've been unsuccessful in catching and holding the eye of someone you find attractive, answer the questions on this checklist honestly. They can help you evaluate whether your eye movements are inadvertently turning others off.

☐ Are your eyes moving lightly and playfully around the flirting triangle? Lay a heavy look on an unsuspecting prospect and it will hang on him like a wet sack. Lively, energetic eyes look eager and interested. Dull, gawking looks make others eager ... to get out of your range!

☐ Have you checked to see whether the person you're flirting with is flirting back? A perfectionist I know once told me about the first time she drove a car. She was so concerned about using the clutch, moving the gearshifts, hitting the gas, and using the right directional lights that she completely missed the stop sign at the corner of her street. Why am I telling you this? Because flirts—particularly new ones—become so involved with their own smiles, looks, and lines that they overlook any smiles, looks, and lines they get in return!

A shared look—that awkward meeting of the eyes that says, "Oops! We caught each other looking!"—always takes one by surprise. It's human nature, then, for the object of your flirtation to look away briefly after catching your glance. But look again. Is he taking a moment to consider your overture, then seeking your eye again? Is she holding your glance just a little longer than necessary? This is no time to reassess your technique. You *are* flirting! It doesn't matter if your skills are unpolished. Someone is obviously seeing you for the gem you are.

☐ Think about the length of your glance. Are you holding it long enough, but not too long? It's easy enough to tell. A long-enough look says, "I see you. Do you see me?" It should last about as long as it would take you to make that statement aloud.

A too-long look, on the other hand, goes on and on like a bad joke. And its effect is nearly the same. The person you are scrutinizing may start to shift in his chair. (And why not? Your staring has put him on the hot seat!) She may shuffle her feet, look back at you suspiciously, or move away from you altogether.

In this depersonalizing society, where people actually learn to avoid each other's gaze, a little bit of eye contact goes a long way. By using the entire flirting triangle as your target, you minimize the possibility of putting your partner on the defensive—and maximize the probability of making a connection.

The object is to catch the gaze of a man or woman you find interesting, linger awhile, then look away. Do this once and you will establish your identity in your partner's mind. Do it several times (without lechery, please!) and your new acquaintance will begin to think of you as a friendly, familiar, and intriguing face in the crowd.

Remember: lingering looks are inviting. If you catch your partner sneaking a peek at you, then looking away, or if you notice that your eyes are meeting more and more often, your invitation has been received and accepted.

Two warnings, though. First, looking at and away too quickly can make your eyes appear darting or sneaky. Beady eyes are scary; bedroom eyes are sensuous, slower.

Finally, please note that the flirting triangle stops at the chin—and so should your eyes! Flirting is all about exploration. But examining the goods below your partner's neck not only sends a cheap, rude message, it can be embarrassing to boot. Not long ago, a friend told me about a female flirt she knew who claimed, teasingly, that she "always measured a man by the size of his wallet." You might think, as I did, that this woman was something of a gold digger. As it turned out, "wallet" was her euphemism for the male derrière. Her penchant for this body part seemed harmless enough ... until one day she got caught with her eyes where they shouldn't be and was immediately confronted not by the man, but by his wife! She was so humiliated by the experience, she swore off Buxton-watching forever.

Of course, none of us is a saint. From time to time, we all succumb to the temptation to take a closer look at the attributes that make others attractive to us. But eyeballing the merchandise isn't good flirting. If you can't be a good flirt, at least be a careful one.

THE WORLD SMILES WITH YOU

Nora hails from a friendly, say-hi-to-everyone kind of town in the Midwest. She adjusted easily to New York's skyscrapers and to the hustle and bustle of city life. But she simply couldn't get over my belief that smiling was an acquired skill. "I just don't get it," Nora said. "To me, reminding people to smile is a bit like reminding them to breathe!"

Needless to say, Nora had attracted more than her share of available men in her first few weeks in the city. But for the rest of us, adopting the right social smile doesn't come as naturally. Afraid that strangers will take our friendliness as a sign of näiveté or a sexual come-on, we censor our facial expressions, saving the most congenial ones for people we can be congenial with safely. But as I explained to Nora, social smiling *is* a skill—and what we as flirts need to acquire is the ability to smile in an easy, approachable way.

Smiles are like greetings cards—there is one for every occasion. We smile when we squeeze past someone in a tight space, as if to say, "I'm sorry, but you know how crowded this room is." We smile sheepishly when the bank teller lets us know that we've overdrawn a checking account. The embarrassed smile we adopt when we're caught looking at a stranger in an elevator apologizes for us. It says, "Sorry you saw me staring; I'll look away now." And I always let a sympathetic smile do the talking for me when I encounter my neighbor cleaning up after his dog. That way I don't have to come right out and say, "There's nothing like a pooper scooper law to put a damper on a beautiful morning!"

Of course, for the Master Flirt, smiles are not so mundane. They are tools that enable him or her to transcend cultural differences, soothe away shyness, and even overcome language barriers without saying a word. For me, no one illustrates that point better than Nathan, a man who enrolled in my group while recovering from a painful breakup with a longtime girlfriend. Nathan didn't contribute much in class. Nor did he show much interest in trying out my techniques—until he booked what he called "a therapeutic trip to Paris." Though he left despondent and unable to speak a word of French, he returned full of energy and anticipation. He just couldn't wait to show me his photos . . . of the Eiffel Tower, the gang at the hotel, and his new acquaintance, Marie.

I met Marie three months later, when she visited Nathan in Manhattan. "The French say Americans smile perhaps too much," she told me. "At first, Nathan and I smiled because we couldn't speak each other's language. Now that I've learned a little English and Nathan speaks a little French, we do it because we're happy."

Birds may not do it; bees may not do it; but Master Flirts routinely use smiles to establish a bond without exchanging a word. And that's where the birds and bees come in. Whether by instinct or education, a good flirt knows that those of us from happy, supportive families were weaned on smiles that wrapped us in love and acceptance like a security blanket. When you're flirting, your goal is to pass that sense of well-being on to others, to make human contact without saying a word, and to send this message of friendliness and warmth: "I may not know you well, but I like you. I'm making this first gesture in the hope that you'll let me know you better."

CHARMING VERSUS CHESHIRE

"Ugh! Rick is smiling like a used-car salesman!" "Don't bare your teeth, Kate, you look like you're going to bite somebody." "That's not a grin . . . it's a leer!"

Smile night at my workshop always brings down the house. It also brings about a keener awareness of the way our lips and teeth work for or against us in social encounters.

It may be arguable that any kind of smile is better than a frown (and some of my seminar attendees have argued just that), but most flirts learn quickly that there's more to smiling than silently saying "cheese." Show too much gum, for example, and you can seem desperate. Grit your teeth and you look maniacal. Seal your lips and bring them up at the corners and you run the risk of resembling the ubiquitous happy face that haunted us through the '60s.

Because you don't have the benefit of your own workshop—and the opinions of thirty scathingly honest singles to guide you—I suggest that you head for the nearest mirror before trying your most flirtatious smile out in public. Think about the message you wish to send, then give yourself the warmest, friendliest, "I'm-a-hot-tomatoest" smile you've got. Now hold that pose. Does your expression look sincere—or painfully fake? Do your lips turn up at the corners or have you captured yourself in some sort of half-hearted grimace? Now check out your eyes. Do they look as though they are smiling, too? Or do they simply look beady and squinty? If you aren't sure, ask a good friend to comment on your demeanor. Many of my seminar graduates entered the workshop either grinning like Cheshire cats or smiling through lips that were sealed as tightly as Tutankhamen's tomb. After listening to the uncensored comments of their peers, they all loosened up—lips first.

And since we're on the subject of lip-lock, let me just make this point: masterpiece or not, Mona Lisa wouldn't get far in today's singles market. In 1992, Rembrandt has become a tooth whitener—and smiling means showing off a double row of clean, healthy-looking teeth. When you approach an interesting prospect, be sure to part your lips and let those pearly whites show. Opening your mouth lets the rest of the world know that you are open to conversation, to flirtation—or to whatever else is on the agenda.

Our facial expressions, like our gestures, can be culturally ingrained or simply a matter of habit. For that reason, the most engaging, natural-looking smiles don't always come naturally to us. In my seminars, I ask my students to flip through fashion magazines to find a model whose smile they particularly admire. Once they have analyzed just what it is about that million-dollar mouth that appeals to them, I suggest that they give it a quick try-on. Of course, someone else's smile is less likely to fit than someone else's jeans, so this exercise is always loads of laughs. But it does make the group aware of the difference among broad grins, pouty looks, and smiles that are sultry, seductive, distant, or cold—and they can adapt their own looks accordingly.

For your own lesson in smile awareness, rent a videotape and watch your favorite actors at work. (To enhance the power of this exercise, I suggest that you choose among movies from an era when expression was everything and sex was fade-to-black.) What are their smiles like? How do their expressions change when the actors are flirting? What does each of their smiles say to you?

Once you've analyzed what makes different kinds of smiles work, ask a friend to shoot a roll of film while you try on an array of smiling looks. Then ask others—particularly friends of the opposite sex—which of the expressions look best on you. You can choose the smile that says precisely what you want it to say, then go to the mirror and practice until you make that smile your own.

One more thing: putting a little uplift on your mouth

has a great side effect. Studies have shown that simply by smiling—even on those days when a smile does not come naturally—you can actually make yourself feel happier. And no one can resist a cheerful, gregarious flirt!

MESSAGES: MIXED AND MISREAD

Annie and Felicia decided to go out to a restaurant together. Felicia chose a spot that was a popular singles hangout. Annie, who was tired of the singles scene, was not happy with this choice. The club, she complained, was a meat market, and she was taking a sabbatical from men. Nevertheless, Felicia won out—and the next thing Annie knew, she was seated at a highly visible table near two men who were clearly enjoying the view.

And so was Felicia. As soon as the men glanced over, she turned toward them, parted her lips slightly, and gave them a small, quick smile. That, to Annie, was bad enough, but when one of the men moved forward in his chair as if he intended to join them, Annie sprang into defensive action. Pressing her lips tightly together, she signaled her displeasure with a taut, inflexible scowl. Her message—a curt "I'm not interested"—hit the target. The man sank back into his chair.

But Felicia was not so easily discouraged. Feeling flirtatious, determined to derail Annie's anti-male train of thought, Felicia turned toward the men again, this time treating them to a full-blown, parted-lip social smile. And as a seductive final fillip, she let her tongue lightly brush the roof of her mouth.

The men were, of course, confused by the mixed messages. The one who had approached returned a tentative smile as if to say, "I'd like to come over but I'm not really sure I should." With that, Felicia nodded and continued to display her winning smile. Sure enough, the men worked their way over to the table. Annie eventually lightened up and a good time was had by all.

There are two amazing aspects to this story. One is that Annie and Felicia are still friends. The other is that the whole introductory "conversation"—from Annie's "not interested" to Felicia's "I'm very interested" to the man's "I'm not sure whether I'm supposed to be interested or not"—was conducted entirely with smiles, gestures, and movements of the lips.

But the best news for good flirts is that seemingly unique experiences like these can and do take place every day. All you have to do is capture and maintain a smile that says, "I'm an interesting person—and right now I'm interested in you," and you have developed a never-fail technique for making these astounding encounters happen—with anyone you choose, anyplace you happen to be.

Of course, the story could have ended another way. Annie could have frightened the men off altogether. She and Felicia could have come to blows over the lobster bisque. The man in question might even have misinterpreted Felicia's invitation to "come on over" as a come-on of another sort—and with date rape at an all-time high that's a possibility that bears consideration.

Certainly there are men who will take any sign of encouragement from a woman as confirmation that she has sex on her mind. And believe it or not, I have spoken to more than a few men who make it a policy to resist overtly seductive women because they don't want to feel pressured into sex with a virtual stranger.

One warning. Smiling in a dark alley, on a deserted street at 3 A.M., in a shady neighborhood, or in questionable districts of foreign countries is not smart. Good flirts are intelligent and appropriate in using their skills. Make sure to flirt in public, safe places.

Does that mean you should refrain from smiling? Absolutely not. The next person you meet may be your significant other! Get rid of a time-wasting lecher by telling him point-blank that *he* made a mistake, then walk away.

If, on the other hand, your smiles are frequently misread, there may be a problem in transmittal rather than reception. Take a closer look at your smiling face in the mirror or ask the advice of friends you go out with regularly. Is your expression overtly seductive or just intriguing enough? Whatever you decide, this Golden Rule of Flirting will never steer you wrong: Smile at others the way you want them to smile at you. If you're comfortable with the looks you're getting, you're doing something right!

FLIRTING FROM HEAD TO TOE

Remember the old song that goes, "You put your whole self in, you take your whole self out"? (Admit it—you've probably even danced to it at other people's weddings.) Well, the Hokey Pokey is just that: hokey. But unless you put your whole self into your flirting, you may be taking your whole self out of the running for the most attractive prospects available to you.

We've all known people who seem to draw others like magnets. We've watched them glide easily into a crowded room, chat effortlessly with whomever they choose, and draw in the most attractive partygoers like bumblebees to honey.

Obviously, if you're hugging the walls while all this is going on, your prospects are ... engaging others and ignoring you. Look closely. Is Ms. Popularity standing straight and stiff like an armed security guard? No! Her spine is flexible and relaxed as if she is at ease with the world. And how about Mr. Life-of-the-Party? Are his shoulders hunched, his arms crossed tightly across this chest? Never! With his arms free to gesture, his posture confidently erect, he knows that hanging loose is a surefire way to make others want to hang around with him.

I know that flirting can be an angst-producing pastime, especially for a fledgling. But the way you put your whole self into a flirting opportunity has a great deal to do with how much you'll ultimately get out of it. It's crucial, then, that you separate the jitters you feel from the body language you display.

Whether it's a dinner party, a singles get-together, or just a night out at the local pub, take a moment from the next social event you attend to catch yourself in what is a typical posture for you. Is there tension in your posture? Are you unconsciously leaning away from the person you're conversing with? You may be talking a good line but your body language is saying, "I'm a cool and distant person. Don't try to get too close." And what if you catch yourself sitting with your legs tightly crossed or your arms folded over your chest? Your anxiety is so obvious, you may as well be wearing a sign that says, "I'm afraid. Don't come near me."

It isn't easy to adopt a comfortable, approachable stance when you aren't feeling comfortable in your surroundings. As a man in my seminar once confessed, "You know how some people are social drinkers? Well, I'm a social hand-wringer." I've seen many first-time flirts try to disguise their anxiety by flinging themselves across a seat like last year's coat. All they accomplish is trading a nervous, strung-out look for a lazy, worn-out one. If parties put you on the edge of your seat, I suggest you get out of your chair altogether. Take a walk—and while you're at it, treat yourself to a few deep breaths. If you have a tendency to fidget with your hands, find something to hold—like a glass or even a crunched-up napkin. But no cigarettes, please. Some potential flirting partners will interpret your smokescreen as a desire to hide. Others will simply find it offensive.

MIRROR, MIRROR . . .

People tend to like people who are like them. Being or becoming in synch is a goal for attracting and relating to others and can be achieved by discovering commonalities with other people. Commonality is generally believed to be best achieved verbally. "Where did you go to school?" "Do you like golf?" "I have a subscription to the ballet, do you like classical dance?" "Oh, do you know Tom? I do too—great guy." But we can learn much from sales and management trainers and communication experts. In the single world, where time and patience is limited, nonverbal communication establishes commonality and builds rapport more quickly than words, simply through a technique called "mirroring," which is the matching of nonverbal body language.

Subtly done, mirroring transmits two positive messages at once. The first is, "I like you." The second, and the most important, is, "I am *like* you." Nothing you can say or show to a potential friend or lover will give you greater, more immediate bonding power.

Mirroring, matching, or mimicking another's gestures, stance, or facial expression is a mating ritual that is not new, and dates back beyond the flirtation of Adam and Eve. Early anthropologists observed matching behaviors in chimpanzees and other socially evolved primates! And if you tune in to the body language of happily married couples you know, you may see an example of mirroring in action. Emotionally bonded couples routinely stand at the same time, lean toward each other at the same moment, or display unconscious facial expressions and physical gestures that are so similar, they can drive us independent singles to distraction.

Of course, mirroring behavior isn't always unconscious. Because it is so effective a tool for building instant rapport, it has become a mainstay in building rapport for therapists and counselors. And because it is a strategy that builds feelings of synchronicity while subtly flattering the person who is being imitated, mirroring is a technique that separates the sweep-you-off-your-feet flirts from the rest.

Here's how it goes. Tamara leans forward across the table, letting her chin rest on her raised hand. Seconds later, her companion, David, does the same. Encouraged by David's willingness to enter her space, Tamara lowers her voice, speaking in a hushed, private tone. David responds in kind. Tamara circles her wine glass with her middle finger; David circles his. Although Tamara clearly likes David, the closeness of the encounter is making her a little uncomfortable. Maintaining a smile, she tilts her head sideways, lifts her wine glass, and swirls her drink playfully. David smiles back raises his glass, and similarly swishes his white wine, mimicking Tamara's motion.

Whoever said, "imitation is the sincerest form of flattery" certainly knew about body language—and human nature. Allowing your chin to rest in your hand doesn't seem like the ultimate romantic gesture. But by following Tamara's lead, David let his companion know that it was important to him to get into her personal habits—and by leaning with her toward the center of the table, he sent the unmistakable message that he was willing to share her personal space as well. At that point, Tamara capitulated and leaned back in her seat. She needed a few moments to get used to the increasing intimacy. Ever the savvy date, David allowed her to retreat. Still, he held her smile as if to say, "Any way you want it, it's okay with me." And when he mimicked her play with the glass, it was as good as telling Tamara, "I like you, I feel in tune with you, and I'm interested in getting more of the same."

My faith in mirroring is unshakeable. I believe it can enhance your career, expand your social circle, and make you a more successful communicator. Remember, as you flirt, he/she doesn't know you but does know and trust himself/herself. By making yourself more like this person, you let him/her know that you share interests, empathize with feelings, care about his/her needs and can be trusted to do something about them. You become a person to get to know.

Voice, too, is important in building rapport. If she's a bottom-line kind of lady who lives by facts and figures, she won't be impressed by your sing-song tone, melodious metaphors, and deep resonant voice. Or if he's the romantic, poetic type, he probably won't like your staccato speech and fast-paced monotone as you graphically represent your financial acumen. But if you can subtly match the timbre and tone of another person's voice, flow into the rhythm of her speech pattern, speed or slow your pace according to his, talk loudly or softly as she does, you can show that person that you are in synch and on their wave length. And if you can further follow his nonverbal lead, mirroring postures and echoing key words as though they were your own, you will make a positive connection.

I cannot emphasize often enough, however, that mirroring is a *subtle* technique. Your movements should never seem contrived or obvious, nor should you attempt to replicate exactly an acquaintance's every gesture. We all have little flaws we don't necessarily want to see in the mirror. No man or woman will be flattered by an admirer who reflects both her positive and negative attributes. If she is slouching in her chair, rest comfortably but confidently in yours. If he mumbles like he has a mouthful of marbles, mimic his volume and his tenor, but not his verbal ineptitude. People can be very self-conscious about their nervous habits. Replicating a new friend's lip-chewing or nail-biting is the kind of flattery that really will get you nowhere. Remember, there is a fine line between mirroring and *aping*. Cross that line and you will come off as dishonest and manipulative. If you aren't sure how far you should go with this very powerful technique, practice the mirroring exercise I've described on page 62, or ask a good friend to indulge you while you learn this new skill. Your movements should reflect your interest in the relationship—not your ability to push someone else's buttons. Indeed, our physical bearing gives away a great deal of information about us, and we need to transmit this information with nuance and depth—just like the spoken word.

The many ways in which we use our bodies to speak for us have intrigued sociologists, kinesiologists, and sexologists for years. And I am happy to report that there have been some recent results that should be of particular interest to male flirts.

MALE CALL

New studies indicate that women send out more signals to pick up men than men do to pick up women. The trouble is that many men don't know how to read the invitations that come their way. Check it out. Is she playing with her hair, tossing her head, or fidgeting with her skirt? These gestures may seem like nervous habits, but they are often a sign that a woman senses sexual tension—or chemistry—between you. Is she smoothing her collar or checking her lipstick? Is her palm open, her skirt hiked slightly higher than before? Does she pout or lick her lips? These are preening behaviors, and they're a sure sign she wants to be looking good the next time you glance her way.

VISUAL, AUDIAL, TACTILE YOU

Jennifer was a clothing designer and artist who specialized in handpainted accessories. She was also a natural, enthusiastic flirt. While other students were still mulling over the basic skills (or gathering the guts to use them), Jennifer was already putting them into practice with great success ... until one night she met a man who totally confounded her.

"It was no problem getting Danny to come over—one smile was all it took. But once I did, his hands were all over me! First he wanted to feel the jacket I'd painted. While he was at it, he fingered the scarf I'd just finished. But when he started running his fingers over my purse, I headed for the door!" Jennifer shook her head. "What is he—a purse-snatcher or just some kind of weirdo?"

For all I knew, her acquaintance could have been with the EPA and was checking the paint for lead. But as I told Jennifer, there is another explanation for Danny's rampant case of the touchy-feelies.

There is a school of neurolinguistics which operates on the premise that each of us has an innate sensory preference on which we rely for stimulation, the transmittal of information, and even emotional fulfillment. To simplify, those of us who are most stimulated by what we see are visual people. Those of us who are more tuned in to what we hear have an aural preference. Tactile people, like Danny, simply cannot help letting their fingers do the walking because they prefer to experience life through the sense of touch.

While I believe that most of us enjoy blending all three preferences, it isn't uncommon to discover an unusually strong visual, aural, or tactile tendency in the people we meet. Nor is such a leaning difficult to identify. People with charisma seem to enjoy all three senses and relate to us in all three modalities.

USE YOUR COMMON SENSES

If you can key in on which sense your potential date relies, you can tailor your communication to his preference and give him a pitch he can't resist.

Barbara has a knack for reading nonverbal clues and honed her skills at her first office job. She was still in the typing pool when she noticed that each of her colleagues routinely surrounded themselves with tools of the trade that were compatible with their sensory preferences. By the time she was ready to move up and out to another company, she had applied her knowledge of communication style to her social life so well that her words never fell on deaf ears, and her flirtations never went unnoticed.

"You can always spot a visual person," Barbara explained to me. "He's the one who can't explain anything to you without drawing you a picture. She's the one who insists that you picture a situation, 'see' what she is saying, or examine this and tell her what you think. In a social situation, it won't do you much good to ask a 'seer' to listen to your idea. They're from the 'show me state'—even if it is a state of mind.

"Aural types may give themselves away by their body language. They lean across the table as if they're straining to hear you. They may even close their eyes or turn away so that what they see won't get in the way of what they might hear. They say that things 'click for them' or 'sounds good.' And what are they listening so hard for? Clues. If they hear a sigh, they want to know if it means you're bored, tired, or frustrated. But most of all, they are listening for your response. They want to know if an idea 'sounds as good' to you as it does to them, or if you are hearing the messages they send.

"But for sheer entertainment value, no one beats the kinetic type. They pace, they gesture, they may even touch. and because they are truly 'hands-on' people, they want you to touch, too—their hand, their new jacket, anything!—just so you can 'get a feel' for what they are all about and a 'sense' of what they are after."

But how can you determine a complete stranger's sensory preference? Barbara has provided the following guidelines. A visual person's surroundings may not be neat, but they are generally orderly and attractive. His credo is, if the pictures are hanging straight on the wall, all is right with the world. To the audial person, the telephone is literally a lifeline. The phone is never more than a short reach away. As for the touchy-feelies of the world, you can pick them out by the texture of their clothes, the energy in their handshakes, the emotionally appealing photographs on their desks, and sometimes, their movements. (Especially that pacing!)

Tony Robbins, the well-known lecturer and millionaire business guru, believes that body language is the secret for tipping the scales in your favor. And so do I.

And if you still doubt that body language either adds to or subtracts from your ultimate marketability, consider this. Researchers have found that 7 percent of what is transmitted comes to us through words or content; 38 percent of the messages we send are communicated by the tone and timber of our voices. The rest of what we say—a whopping 55 percent of our total communication—is transmitted to others through unconscious gestures and manipulation of the body.

You don't have to be a mathematical whiz to see how this data adds up. A smart flirt who projects his voice and displays his bearing in a positive way is communicating at 93 percent of his capacity without ever saying a word! And the remaining 7 percenters? They may be all talk, but they aren't likely to get any action.

CLOSE ENCOUNTERS OF THE FLIRTATIOUS KIND

How do you get to Carnegie Hall with the date of your dreams? Practice, practice, practice! These simple exercises will help you incorporate the flirting fundamentals into your day-to-day life. Don't be surprised if they make a wonderful difference in the way you spend your evenings!

A STRONG, SILENT STRATEGY

Pretend you are a journalist writing an article on flirting skills. Begin your research by watching couples in action. Observe their body language, eye contact, the little gestures that speak louder than words. Which couples are really into each other? Which are just filling an empty space on their social calendar? If you aren't sure, send out some nonverbal signals of your own and see what happens. Be sure to keep them discreet, though. You won't be able to maintain your journalistic silence if you're forced to do some hasty explaining!

ACTING OUT

Ask a few friends to join you in a game of charades, but instead of guessing movie titles or slogans, use emotions instead. Write a variety of emotional responses on separate slips of paper (try anger, happiness, arrogance, shyness, fear, triumph, pleasure, hostility, desire, disgust, and surprise for starters), then pay attention while each person takes a turn acting out his or her choice. How does one player use his lips to communicate disgust, fear, or arrogance? How does another use her eyes to convey happiness, desire, and pleasure? Of course, you should play the game for fun—but the flashes of insight you gain will make flirting more fun, too.

THE FACE IN THE MIRROR

Draw a triangle on a mirror. Inside, sketch two eyes, a nose, and a mouth. Practice moving your eyes all around the target area, from forehead to chin, from temple to temple, glancing only occasionally into the eyes. This exercise is not only a great stare-diffuser, it's great practice for all those times you need to make effective eye contact—whether on the job, on the street, or in a flirting situation.

ME AND MY SHADOW

Ask a friend to speak for three minutes on the subject of his choice. As he does, mimic every gesture, movement, or expression he makes. Then have him do the same while you hold forth. The purpose of this exercise is twofold. First, it allows you to take an honest look at the unconscious gestures in your own repertoire. Second, it gives you a chance to practice subtle mirroring—a powerful skill for developing immediate rapport.

HINTS FOR THE BACK-TO-BASICS FLIRT

Remember:

- Your body is speaking even when you're not. Be aware of the message you are sending.
- A good flirt can always get by on the Big Three: intriguing eyes, smiling lips, and effective body language.
- Look for nonverbal signals when trying to determine whether someone is interested in you.
- "Flirt" is a friendly verb. Use your eyes in a playful way.
- The Flirting Triangle stops at the chin. No peeking!
- Keep the jitters you feel out of the image you project.
- Imitation is the sincerest form of flattery. Use mirroring to reflect your interest in a flirting partner.
- Smile, smile, smile! Someone is interested in you!

4

WHAT TO SAY
AFTER YOU'VE
SAID HELLO

—

"When do I usually run into conversational trouble? That's easy. I say hi. Then I'm in trouble." —LAURA, age 21

When was the last time you initiated a pleasant conversation with a complete stranger? Think about it.

This question has become a mainstay of my singles seminars—and certainly not because of the lively response it evokes. In fact, as soon as I ask it, all I hear is a few moans and groans and maybe one or two pleading answers. ("I never start conversations. that's my problem!") Then the room becomes totally silent.

The truth is, we all engage strangers in conversation nearly every day, without even thinking about it. But because these impromptu meetings take place without thought, planning, or risk, we tend to overlook them, as though they just don't count. That's why some of my workshops become as quiet as a cloister! Most singles are so fixed on the daunting task of intriguing that special someone with just the right banter (or on their fear of looking silly if they can't), they simply can't recall the last time they charmed someone who, to them, was not so special, like the elevator operator, the upstairs neighbor, the mail carrier, or anyone else they did not think about in sexual terms.

One salesman in the group, who made his living by talking to strangers, claimed that he never approached women to whom he had not been introduced. When I reminded him that he had made a lot of cold cash by warming up clients of the opposite sex, he clarified his feelings this way. "Oh, I can talk to *any* client," he announced proudly. "Even those who aren't remotely interested in what I'm selling. But picking up a conversation with a woman I find attractive ..." He shook his head. "That's a little too risky for me."

IS YOUR DOUBLE STANDARD KEEPING YOU SINGLE?

It might be if you're chatting up the butcher, the baker, and the local matchmaker and ignoring that hot prospect at the taxi stand.

Obviously, there are fewer risks involved in conversing with a person in whom we have little interest. Our egos and libidos aren't invested in any particular outcome. And because we tend to keep those contacts light and unemotional, there is little chance of hurt feelings on either side. For some of us, speaking to an anonymous person whom we don't find attractive can even be an ego boost. To put it plainly, we find it easier to speak to people in passing because we've already decided to pass on them.

If you've been saving your best conversation for insignificant encounters with people who don't interest you, you are cheating yourself out of countless opportunities to meet that significant other. And if you are fearful that your efforts to engage others in spontaneous conversation will impress some fuddy-duddies as being too aggressive, too personal, or too desperate, or simply insane, remember this: by maintaining your silence, you are guaranteed not to impress them at all. And that's not effective flirting!

Now don't get the wrong idea. I'm not saying that talk is cheap. I'm saying that spontaneous conversation should be given out absolutely free—especially to those special people who intrigue us most. And we *can* give it freely, once we've transcended our unfounded fears, stranger anxiety, and serious intent.

BREAKING THE SILENCE BARRIER

Karen was a seminar recruit who had described herself at our first meeting as "terminally tongue-tied." But when I asked her to reveal the emotions behind her silence, her tongue loosened up considerably.

"What am I afraid of? Do you want the short list or do we have time to go through the complete catalog?"

She laughed with the rest of the group, then continued. "Most of the time, I'm afraid that the person I've chosen to talk to won't find me attractive and he won't talk back. Even on 'good hair days' when I'm feeling more confident about my appearance, I worry that I'll say something stupid and he *still* won't talk back. If he's standing on a corner reading a paper or seems engrossed in something, I convince myself that idle chatter would interrupt his train of thought. In that case, I'm afraid that he *might* talk back— like Archie Bunker—and tell me to stifle."

By the end of Karen's monologue, the entire group was laughing—not at Karen, but at themselves. Karen hadn't just revealed her own conversation-killing fantasy, she had described everyone else's, too. In our minds, other people are always dazzlingly attractive, even in triple-digit humidity. We look bedraggled. When other people converse, they combine the easy style of Oprah Winfrey, the vocabulary of William F. Buckley, and the intelligence of William Safire. We're somewhere between Edith Bunker and Professor Irwin Corey. Why do other people always know the right thing to say when we don't dare open our mouths? We think our feet are in there!

No wonder singles can live in cities where they are literally elbow to elbow with millions of people every day and still report that they can't meet anybody. Everyone is afraid to speak first!

If you are shy or anxious, or if you find yourself rerunning your own version of Karen's conversational nightmare, it should be reassuring to know that you are in good company. Most people are just as anxious about encountering strangers as you are. (Why do you think you see so many otherwise intelligent, good-looking singles peeking out at you from behind the morning newspaper? Or staring fixedly at the elevator buttons throughout a thirty-story ride? They're hiding!) But that doesn't mean *you* have to participate in a silent standoff.

The good news is this: for every woman hoping that some significant other will break the silence barrier, there is a man who is hoping the same. And for every single man wondering whether that lovely woman would respond to an impromptu greeting, there is a woman with a great smile just waiting for a reason to use it. Most attractive strangers will respond to you. If they've been in your position before, they will appreciate the courage it took for you to speak up. And if your inexperience shows in your speech? All the better! Based on the opinions expressed in my seminars, most singles find a bit of awkwardness charming— and certainly small doses of vulnerability are preferable to staving off a conversational partner who seems too smooth, too aggressive, or too practiced.

GETTING TO HELLO

Of course, not seeming practiced doesn't mean you shouldn't practice at all. We're all most comfortable when we're doing something we've done many times before—and that goes double for reaching out to others in a new way.

According to the men and women in my seminar, this exercise will give you something your mother never gave you: permission to speak to strangers. It will also give you a chance to see for yourself that you *can* start a conversation with anyone, anytime, anyplace.

Start practicing with this easy opener. Each day, say hello to at least ten acquaintances (people who know you by sight, but who are not your personal friends). Congratulate yourself on each positive response you receive. When you feel comfortable, turn your simple greeting into an invitation to converse. You may, for example, say hello, introduce yourself, then ask an open-ended question. ("Hi! My name is Dolores. Isn't this sunshine great after so many days of rain?") When you do, take special notice of the people who seem appreciative of your gesture. Many of the people you pass each day are just dying for a chance to air their views!

When you are able to converse easily with acquaintances, begin making contact with potential partners, people who attract you, or who seem attracted *to* you. How many of them seem pleased that you have made the first move? If your experience is like that of my seminar graduates, you'll notice that people are willing to be as frank with you as you are with them. If you are a woman, you will see that most gentlemen appreciate your making the first move—as they have had to do for so many years. And those realizations, combined with a little self-confidence, can open the door to an exciting new realm of flirting.

TURNING A GREETING INTO A MEETING

"I hate hello. It leads to . . . I don't know where."

If I had not heard it myself, I would have thought that line came from a Woody Allen script. But I did hear it, from a journalist named Richard. Like many writers, Richard believed that his unique charm was something he communicated best on paper—not face to face. And like single people everywhere, he was struggling not with hello, but with what came after it.

"It's a blank page," he said in frustration. "Sure, you want to write on it . . . but where do you begin?"

If I have learned one thing as a lifelong flirt, it is this: almost anything you say to a new prospect, short of being rude, sarcastic, or outright insulting, is good flirting. In my seminars, how to break the ice is always a hot topic. In the eight years I've spent teaching, I've heard of men who were absolutely bowled over by women who asked for something as simple as a pencil, directions, or the use of an umbrella in a sudden shower. And I've known women who absolutely melted when asked whether it was hot enough for them, whether they thought it would snow, or how to remove the giblet bag from a turkey—after it was cooked. (I even know one woman who met her soon-to-be husband when he demanded her measurements! Of course, he *is* a tailor . . .)

The lesson is this: when it comes to getting over the "hello hurdle," *any inane remark will do.*

Lydia met the man in her future at a charity event. He was tucked behind a pole, and she curiously peeked around to see who belonged to the fancy reptile cowboy boots. Caught staring, she looked at his cream-colored drink and said the first thing that came into her head, "What are you drinking?"

"Sombrero," he replied.

"What's a sombrero?" she asked.

"Kahlúa and milk," he answered. And so the conversation went. He loved sweet drinks; she asked a lot of questions, and finally he asked the important one. "Are you free for a wine-tasting Friday night?"

As long as you're not being just plain dumb, the more inane your remark the better! Okay . . . so maybe you've got a preference for scintillating talk. But until you get warmed up, small talk is a big opportunity. It isn't threatening, depressing, or serious. It isn't intellectually or emotionally taxing. All it is, is a little touch of humanity in a busy, bustling world. And who couldn't stand a little more of that?

As for a place to start, I'll tell you just what I told Richard. It's best to begin right where you are, by taking notice of and commenting on what's going on around you. And the most effective way to get in touch with that—and with others—is to go back to a lesson learned by all fledgling writers.

THE FIVE W'S

❤ *Who* is that compelling person who caught your eye in the grocery checkout line? If what he is wearing or what she is carrying reveals something about him or her, the object of your flirtation has given you an easy in. Jump on it!

Does that athletic-looking guy in the warm-up suit know the best jogging track in the city? Ask him! Could that pulled-together businesswoman recommend a quiet local restaurant for an important client meeting you've got coming up? Find out! Maybe you'll get her card while you're at it.

One woman in my seminar began a happy relationship with a plainclothes police detective when he investigated a burglary at her home. She noticed—somewhat suspiciously—that he wasn't in uniform. After showing her his badge, he noticed her assets.

● *What* are you doing? If you've been following my advice, you're getting out of the house on a regular basis. And if you're getting out of the house, you're engaging in some form of social activity. Take advantage of it! Any organized activity—whether it's a hobby class, a trade show, or a seminar in flirting—offers you countless opportunities to ask questions, offer advice, or speak about what you're learning to the people around you.

When you stop to think about it, even those so-called "solitary" pursuits don't have to be so solitary if you are willing to share your private thoughts with others. Skiing solo? Comment on the length of the lift line. Shopping for hardware? Ask a fellow browser to explain the difference between a ball-peen hammer and a carpenter's mallet.

It only takes a few friendly words to bring the people around you into your experience. You can decide later whether to make them a part of your life.

● *Where* are you? The city I live in, New York City, is a flirt's paradise. That's because there are so many out-of-the-ordinary things happening on the streets that you simply can't keep your comments to yourself.

You may live in a place where window washers hang twenty-three floors above the ground. Or you may be in a cozy small town where people still hang their laundry in the sun. But if you are missing the more unique aspects of everyday life you are overlooking countless opportunities to reach out and impress someone with a clever observation, a witty remark, or a helping hand.

Still find yourself doubting that the world can be your flirting prop? This L.A. story should change your mind. A friend of a friend of mine found herself gridlocked in one of Los Angeles's most frustrating everyday occurrences: a traffic jam. Going nowhere fast, she had plenty of time to notice the people in the cars around her, particularly Mr.

RX-7 in the Mazda beside her. For fifteen minutes, this Master Flirt watched as the man in the sports car craned his neck, checked his watch, and pounded the steering wheel. Then she took pity on him. Rolling down her window, she waved the antenna of her car phone like a wand and said, "I've made my morning appointments disappear. Now how about you?" To make a long story short, he used her phone *and* took her number—all because she was willing to enjoy being where she was and share the experience with someone around her. Otherwise, Mr. Mazda would surely have disappeared in a cloud of exhaust.

♥ *Why* and *When*. I know you aren't supposed to answer a question with a question. But Why and When are the perfect answers to the question, "How am I supposed to make conversation with a complete stranger?"

From "Why didn't the bus stop at this corner?" to "When does this blasted motor vehicle inspection station open, anyway?", asking for information is a great way to make yourself knowledgeable and approachable. It's also a terrific way to gather info of a more personal kind.

Want to know whether she lives in the neighborhood? If she does, she'll know about the local buses, restaurants, and shops. Wondering whether those children are his? Ask where they go to school. Any parent will surely embellish on that response.

And if that hot prospect turns out to be not so hot after all? You've learned the bus schedule. Just get on board and find someone more suitable to flirt with.

HOW NOT TO END A CONVERSATION

"When it comes to making myself known to an interesting man, I have no trouble breaking the rules of tradition. I just walk right up, introduce myself, and start talking," announced Andi, a straightforward, go-for-it type of flirt with chutzpah to burn. "The problem is, somewhere along the line, the men stop talking back."

"For a while, I was involved with a singles group. I used to tell my friends that it was called the Dysfunctional Dating Service because every man in it was conversationally challenged," Andi continued. "Now I'm wondering if the person with the problem isn't me."

First there's an awkward silence. Then your conversational partner begins staring at the twist of lime floating in her Perrier as if it were a life raft. Finally, she excuses herself, somewhat frantically. She simply must hunt down the hostess, she says, to compliment her on "that wonderful rumaki."

Because we can't watch ourselves in action as we meet and talk to others, it isn't easy for us to diagnose our own communication problems. But the symptoms of conversational bailout are hard to miss. And no matter how tasty the appetizers, knowing that we have said the wrong thing, the dull thing, or the boorish thing always makes us feel like chopped liver.

As you know by now, I'm all for breaking the constraints of tradition—as Andi does—when it comes to flirting. But breaking the rules of good conversation can only result in a breakdown in communication. Worst of all, no amount of eye contact or unrestrained smiling can undo the damage you've done with your mouth.

You've worked so hard to get that dinner party conversation started. Use these simple guidelines and you'll keep it going through dessert!

RULE #1: DON'T BE THE SUNSHINE OF *YOUR* LIFE.

In the past few minutes, you've found out that she loves ballet, hates modern dance, and exercises to (of all things!) rap music. So why isn't she talking? If you are using her interests as a reason to spout your opinions, judge her musical taste, or challenge her viewpoint on the artistic value of rap music, your conversation is not about getting to know her. It's about letting her get to know you.

There's an old joke about conversation: "Well, that's enough talk about me. Let's talk about you. What do *you* think of me?" You'll never know unless you let your conversational partners have their say!

Nature provided you with two ears and one mouth. Use them in the proper proportion and you can learn a lot. And if you're the kind of mingler who works a party with "your story reminds me of something that happened to me" on the tip of your tongue, remember this: the wonder of you is too dazzling to be revealed in the first ten minutes of conversation. Narcissists are lonely hearts. Space out the personal data before the people you meet space out on you.

RULE #2: GIVE COMPLIMENTS FREELY BUT SINCERELY.

If she's impressed you with her knowledge of cubist painting or he's got the warmest smile you've ever seen, say so! Most of us put a great deal of time and effort into our appearance, intellect, and interests. Knowing that those efforts are appreciated gives us a sense of validation—and we, in turn, give big brownie points to those special people who make us feel good.

Of course, that doesn't mean you should lay on the praise with a trowel. Anyone can spot an insincere flatterer at forty paces, and forty paces away is usually where we want those oily types to stay.

If you are uncomfortable with giving compliments or fear your comment will be taken the wrong way, a less personal compliment, like the one a neighbor laid on me, will do.

TJ lives on my street. When I met him one day out walking some twenty blocks from our neighborhood, I asked him what he was doing so far from our usual stomping ground.

TJ checked his watch, smiled, and replied, "I was just waiting for you to pass by. Now I can go home."

With that charming comment, he not only made my day, he made himself more special to me.

However, there is one final distinction that needs to be made before you take your flattering comments to the streets. "You look so cheerful today" is a compliment. "You look like one red-hot mama!" is the opening salvo in a sexual confrontation. Women are justifiably sensitive about being treated as sexual playthings. They will not be receptive to any man's unsolicited comments on their breasts, hips, posteriors, or any other part of the anatomy that falls between the neck and the ankles. Nor should women confuse catcalling, sexually oriented commentary or double entendres with liberation. The men I know find those more embarrassing than titillating—and humiliation is definitely not the way to win points with the opposite sex.

RULE #3: ASK OPEN-ENDED QUESTIONS.

Larry was dying to get to first base with Cyndi, a cute brunette he saw at his creative writing class every Tuesday night. When he told me that he had asked her some questions and gotten nowhere, I inquired what he had asked.

"You know, the usual," he replied. "'Do you like this class?' 'Have you always been interested in writing?' 'Do you have a spare pencil?' That kind of thing."

That kind of thing? No wonder Cyndi didn't seem to think much of Larry. His questions weren't requiring her to think at all!

"Do you enjoy studying writing?" "What do you think of celebrity kiss-and-tell books?" "Andy Rooney says he still writes all of his material on an old Underwood typewriter. How do you prefer to work?" These are the kinds of questions Larry should have asked because they require something other than a yes or no answer. Sure, Cyndi would have had to work at a response, but her answers would have given Larry some idea how her mind and feelings operate. And that kind of personal link is the stuff from which interesting connections, great friendships, and warm relationships are made. Which brings us to this important guideline...

RULE #4: PERSONALIZE THE CONVERSATION.

Lydia dated a man named Frank who was totally absorbed in photography. The problem was this: although she had no interest in the technical aspects of his hobby, she had a great deal of interest in him.

Smart Lydia knew that it would do her no good to question him about apertures, lenses, or long-range focusing. Those weren't the things she cared about. So instead of focusing on the technical, she zoomed in on the personal, using photography as a frame for her fledgling romance. She asked Frank what got him started with photography, how he felt about taking pictures, what subjects turned him on, and how the emotions of his subjects affected his results. In short, she capitalized on the personal, human element behind Frank's favorite subject. And before she knew it, Frank's solitary pursuit wasn't so solitary anymore. He was including her in his photographic journeys and making her privy to his most intimate thoughts.

RULE #5: ENTHUSIASM IS CONTAGIOUS. BE A CARRIER.

Who could resist a stimulating new person whose excitement about her life makes you more enthusiastic about yours? As we saw in the example above, Frank couldn't. And neither can anyone else.

Your passion energizes others. It makes them want to

get onto your wavelength. So save the hangdog looks and gloomy observations for another, less important victim. Be at your conversational best and you'll bring out the best in everyone you meet.

RULE #6: STOP THAT WHINING!

So your boss chewed you out, the apartment you live in is heatless in January, and your ex returned the kids two hours early just to louse up your schedule. We all have enough troubles of our own. We don't need to go out to hear yours.

Misery might love company, but company does not love misery. When you close your door, lock your problems inside. That way, every time you go out you'll be free to enjoy positive relating.

RULE #7: LEARN TO LAUGH AT YOURSELF.

Whether the wind just whipped your $120 perm into a Don King hairdo or you tromped on a dance partner's pumps, social gaffes don't have to be a disaster. Knowing that you are a fallible human being makes others feel more human themselves, more comfortable and relaxed. And that is the essence of successful flirting.

Don't misunderstand me—I'm not suggesting that you put yourself down. But if you can use humor to rise above the little foibles that plague us all, you will show the world that it's okay to be less than perfect. And that can be very appealing to the people around you, who suspect they're not so perfect, either.

RULE #8: CARRY A CONVERSATIONAL AID.

T-shirts, buttons, books, shopping bags, unusual jewelry, dogs, babies, suspenders, flowered ties . . . any object that is visible and worthy of comment will bring out the closet commentator in everyone you meet.

For example, I got months of mileage out of an aircast I wore on my sprained ankle. Not only was it was the perfect conversational opener (men couldn't resist asking how I had hurt myself), it also enabled me to keep the conversation going by adding a little harmless, humorous embellishment to my story. So you see, sprains aside, making small talk really doesn't have to be a painful experience. Even something negative can be a conversation-starter as long as you're not complaining about it.

RULE #9: DON'T CRITICIZE OR JUDGE.

At thirty-eight, Pam thought she had been through it all, including a hasty marriage, a nasty divorce, and a long custody battle. When she met Allen, an older businessman who was going through a custody fight of his own, it seemed like a match made in People's Court. Until her personal judgments cut it short.

"Allen asked me how I came to be the residential parent of my son, Ryan. So I explained that I had always been Ryan's primary caretaker, and that since my ex-husband worked seventy hours a week, I had more time for a child. He seemed okay with that," she recalled. "But then I told him how I really felt—that men don't really understand the needs of small children, and that maybe a two-year-old really was better off with his mother. He went ballistic! First he let me know that his ex-wife only worked twenty hours a week but that she spent another thirty with her boyfriend. Then he told me that he had taken a three-month leave of absence to care for his daughter after his wife abandoned the house. Finally he said that I should keep my sexist opinions to myself. And he made sure I did, too. He never called again."

You never know what's going on in someone else's life

and it's not smart to give an opinion on what you don't know. Certainly a conversational partner who wants to vent on some personal matter should be allowed to do so. Listen and you're sure to learn a lot. But if you're projecting your beliefs onto his or her problem, or putting your two cents in every chance you get, don't be surprised if the conversation and the relationship end abruptly.

RULE #10: NEVER INTERRUPT.

Communication is a two-part process. In the first part, your mouth is open. During the second part, your ears should be open. Cut off a speaker in midsentence (or worse, finish the sentence for him!) and you are not only being rude, you are throwing the communication process out of balance. Or, if you race ahead of your thoughts, thinking of words of wisdom to impress her with next, you might say something truly brilliant—but inappropriate or off her wavelength.

We all like to think we are being heard, that what we are saying is stimulating. (Don't you resent a "listener" who runs off with your story before you've had a chance to finish it?) Although most of us don't pay attention as we should (see Chapter 5 for tips on active listening), interrupting is a dead giveaway that you are less than enrapt. So bite your tongue and listen without judging. As an executive I know put it, "the better we listen, the luckier we get." That good advice doesn't just apply to the boardroom.

HE SAID/SHE SAID

"She asked me what was new, so I told her . . . about my new boss, my new responsibilities, my new desk chair . . ."
—ADAM, age 33

"I talk to my women friends about my kids all the time. But when I brought Stevie's clarinet recital up to a man I met, he seemed to be miles away. Or he was wishing he was."
                                                    —JUNE, age 39

The communication gap between men and women has been the subject of many books and the reason behind many flirtatious failures. At times, it seems as though the conversational difference between the sexes is so deep-rooted it must be chromosomal. (Maybe that's why he tunes out when she tunes into her emotions . . . his Y chromosome reacts with a Yawn.)

Why a woman can't be more like a man (and vice versa) is actually a combination of nature, nurture, and cultural influences. But knowing that won't help you as much as these tips for verbal flirting with the opposite sex will. The pointers below will help you separate the hot topics from subjects that are strictly hands-off.

GUIDELINES FOR MEN

♂ Talk about your emotions. Women don't want mush, but they don't want macho, either. If you find it difficult to come across as sensitive and vulnerable without seeming to cry on a woman's shoulder, ask a woman friend for her opinion. In the interest of women everywhere, she'll be glad to help.

♂ Do ask for advice. She won't be insulted if you ask her opinion on your new Jerry Garcia–designed tie, but if you can ask her for help with your investment portfolio, or your daughter's sassy attitude, so much the better.

♂ Don't kiss and tell. Bragging about your past sexual conquests (even if you don't think you're bragging) makes a woman feel like one of the crowd—not one in a million.

♂   Let her know you're listening. Nod, smile, mumble "uh-huh"—but do something to signal that you're paying attention or validating what she is saying.

♂   Don't patronize her. Calling her "honey" or "dear" or talking down to her as if she were your intellectual inferior will send her off in search of a less sexist companion.

♂   Don't wield knowledge like a club. Maybe her kvetching about the long wait in her dentist's office lets you know that she doesn't understand medical emergencies. Coming in with "I am an oral surgeon with a busy practice and I think..." KO's conversation.

♂   Keep your political speeches, religious zeal, and mentally ill mother to yourself, at least on that all-important first date. Give the other person a chance to like you for yourself and you'll increase the chances that she'll like you despite your differences.

♂   Never ask a woman a question simply to determine her age, such as "How old are your children?" or "What year did you graduate college?" Ageism is very real. No woman wants to be discriminated against because she's too old, too young, or too in-between.

♂   Even if sex is on your mind, keep it off your lips. There is a fine line between humor and distasteful innuendo. The only way you can be sure that you're staying on the safe side of that line is to keep the jokes, double entendres, and come-ons to yourself.

And try to understand that when a woman dresses attractively—or even suggestively—it is not a signal that she is willing to hop into the sack. What may seem like an advertisement to you may be a matter of style to her. If she is trying to attract attention, its probably not sexual attention. Remember: women like sex, but they don't like being sex objects.

GUIDELINES FOR WOMEN

♀ Do talk about your job—especially if you love it. Men find independent, accomplished women fascinating.

♀ Don't ask him what he does for a living or what kind of car he drives until you know him well. These may seem like innocent questions to you, but to him they may translate to "How much money do you make?" Men are very touchy about women who have dollar signs in their eyes. Surprised? Don't be. Men are every bit as put off by being treated as "success objects" as women are by being seen as sex objects. And rightly so.

♀ Bridge the gender gap. Men weren't allowed to speak about their feelings until recently. When he tries, give him encouragement and an A for effort. Meanwhile, it wouldn't hurt you to dabble in a little "malespeak," just to make him comfortable. Golf trivia, automobile maintenance, or home repair topics give you time to build intimacy—and that's what great conversation is all about.

♀ Don't talk about your past. Your reputation as a college party animal or the fifteen years you spent in therapy may seem innocuous to you now, but personal tidbits like these may be too juicy for some men to digest.

♀ Do a sound check. Shrill voices are no thrill. And weak, whispery tones are downright annoying.

If you find you're losing audience after audience, the problem may not be what you say, but the way you say it. Speak into a tape recorder if you're not sure how you sound. Then ask a good friend to listen and comment.

♀ Don't ramble on about your health problems. Did you ever see a medical disaster walking? Well, I did. One night I watched as an otherwise attractive woman put an entire dinner party at dis-ease by chattering on about her bad back, migraines, hypoglycemia, and allergy to red wine. Needless to say, the men kept their distance. She clearly wasn't up to the rigors of a relationship.

♀ Leave your children with the sitter. Or wherever they are. I know, I know. Your kids are a part of you. You and they are a package deal. But the immediate goal of flirting is to find a companion for yourself, not a role model for your children.

One of the best relationships I ever had began during the summer when my kids were away at camp. After two months together, my partner not only liked me, he felt secure enough in our relationship to welcome my children. Ultimately you may find a man who has enough love to give to your entire family, too. But this time and this conversation are just for you. Enjoy!

LET'S HEAR A LITTLE CHATTER OUT THERE!

Practice makes the perfect Master Flirt. Here are some simple exercises that enable you to practice your conversational skills anywhere, anytime, on any silent stranger who seems to need a good talking to.

POOR LITTLE WALLFLOWER

Take pity on those shy souls who haven't had the benefit of this book: make the first move! Remind yourself that the object of your flirtation would love to establish contact, if only he or she had the courage. Give yourself permission to save him or her from isolation, then jump right in the conversational swim.

FOR OPENERS . . .

A simple hello, followed by an open-ended question, is best. Stay away from inquiries that begin with "is," "isn't," "can," or "can't." These are questions that allow people to respond with a simple yes or no. Instead, use conversational openers like these to encourage a new friend to dig deep for answers:

1. How do you feel about _____?
2. I am interested in your point of view. What do you think about _____?
3. I've heard that you're an expert on this sort of thing. What do you think of _____?
4. How did you get involved in this hobby/pastime/cause?
5. What do you consider the perfect evening?
6. What adventures have you had that stand out in your mind?
7. Have you ever encountered a situation like this before?
8. If you won the lottery, what would you buy first, second, and third? (A great icebreaker for that lottery-ticket line!)
9. What traits do you find most appealing in a woman/man?
10. Do you like to travel? (Innocuous enough on the surface, but people are absolutely passionate about traveling. They either love it or hate it.)

HAPPY ENDINGS

The way a conversation ends is every bit as important as the way it began. And whether you've been chatting up the most recent love of your life or extricating yourself from the plague of the party, it is crucial that your good impression follow you out the door. Why? Because good flirts have no investment in making other people feel bad. And because it is silly to burn a bridge you may one day have reason to cross.

On the other hand, there are people who make "It was nice to get to know you" stick in your throat like a glob of peanut butter. In those cases, it may help to focus on the fact that this meeting came about because of your skill as a consummate flirt. And that *is* nice to know.

Whether your retreat is hasty or lingering, here are some neutral closings to ensure that you'll always leave a good impression.

1. Oh, look at the time! I really must be going.
2. I'd love to continue this conversation another time. Is coffee next Thursday good for you?
3. Excuse me, but I see someone I must speak to.
4. I'm going to have a drink at the bar. Catch you later.
5. I really learned a lot from you about [fill in specific topic]. Thanks for the tips!

A SUMMARY FOR SMOOTH- (BUT NOT FAST-) TALKING FLIRTS

Remember:

- Even the most intricate relationships start with a simple hello.
- Never be rude, sarcastic, judgmental, or threatening.
- You have two ears and one mouth. That's nature's way of telling you to listen twice as much as you speak.
- Be generous with sincere compliments.
- Any inane remark, pleasantly phrased, is a good conversation-starter.
- Open-ended questions make people open up to you.
- Don't brag, show off, or make yourself your favorite topic.
- If your past is spicier than the salsa, don't be surprised if others find it hard to swallow.
- Tune in to the interests of others.

5

HOW TO GET
YOUR MESSAGE
ACROSS WITHOUT
SAYING A WORD

Sharon twirls her hair between her fingers. Brian smooths the lapels of his jacket, then leans forward across the table. Sharon tilts her head as she listens to Brian's whispered message. Smiling, she slips her heel out of her pump and lets the shoe dangle from her toe. Brian begins to slowly circle the rim of his wine glass with his index finger.

What's going on here? Is it love? Is it lust? Is it boredom? While an in-depth study of kinesics, or body language, will give you *some* insight into the various cultural and sociological messages behind human movements, the bottom line is that no one really knows what—if anything—each of our movements may mean at a given time.

In the silent love story between Sharon and Brian, for example, Sharon sits with her legs crossed in Brian's direction. Does that mean she's favorably inclined toward him?

Not necessarily. If Sharon is in the habit of crossing her right leg over her left, that's simply the position she would assume even if Attila the Hun were stirring a mai tai with a human bone in the seat beside her. My friend Edna, on the other hand, tends to sit with her back very straight and her chest thrust out. Although some body language "experts" would argue that Edna is demonstrating aggressive behavior by putting her breasts on display, I happen to know that she has worn a back brace for years and has a difficult time sitting in any other position.

Language, by definition, is the communication of thoughts and feelings. And whether it is used consciously or unconsciously, body language *is* a legitimate transmitter of what we need, feel, or think. Some experts even maintain that kinesis is communication in its purest form because it is free of the wordy explanations, confusing second-guesses, and annoying mixed messages that plague us in conversation.

One warning. A single gesture does not tell the whole story. Look for "gesture clusters." If she tosses her head, or he tightens his tie, it does not mean she or he is yours. The wink, the raised eyebrow have meaning, but one signal is not enough. Make no assumptions from arms crossed in front of a chest or a shrug of the shoulder, but combine crossed arms, slouched shoulders, head down, frown, a slow dragging shuffle and a deep sigh, and you can pretty well assume this person is depressed, down, shy or at the very least not interested in making your acquaintance right now. We need to read body language in context and look for a series of signals.

Those of us who believe that spoken language is what separates us from the apes tend to pooh-pooh kinesis as a crude medium that cannot possibly convey the complex nuances of human thought and emotion. Yet infants, who are natural physical linguists, use body language to communicate a surprising range of messages, from the most basic (such as "Feed me *now!*") to the esoteric ("I'm so interested in this, I could just burst!"). It's only natural, then, that as adults we cultivate this survival skill to bring people closer to us or to keep them away.

Of course, some of us still use body language for the most common reason that babies do: to get picked up! And sending that message can be a little more complicated when you're three decades old than it was when you were three months old.

THAT COME-HITHER LOOK

"I know I'm attractive. I was a runway model for seven years—and I've worked hard to stay in shape," said Tricia, a classic beauty at age thirty-five. "So maybe you can tell me why, when I'm out with friends, I'm never the one to get asked to dance. Why am I the one who's always left sitting there like a table decoration?"

You can always tell when a child wants to be held. He or she approaches you with arms wide open. The message is so clear, so unmistakable, that even those of us who have never been parents know that all we have to do to make the child happy is hug back.

Twenty or more years and quite a few rejections later, we still want to be held, but we're no longer willing to wear our needs on our sleeves. Time, it seems, has taught us another survival mechanism: self-protection. We've learned the hard way that too much vulnerability can hurt us, so we hold back and mask our feelings. That kind of masking, as it turned out, was a technique that Tricia had perfected.

One evening, I was lucky enough to be invited out with Tricia and her friends. While having a model at the table turned out to be a great flirting prop for the rest of us, I could see how Tricia came to be viewed just that way—as a prop—by the men in the room. As a model, I suppose, Tricia's oh-so-bored look was part of her mysterious glamour. But with her bubbly, vivacious friends in tow, that chichi-chagrined appearance just made Tricia seem like a drag.

Nor did Tricia's forbidding mask stop at her bateau neckline. While her friends gestured, clapped, and even reached over to the next table to "steal" an attractive man's ashtray, Tricia kept her arms folded firmly over her chest like armor. And when four men finally approached the table (actually, they charged it like a Marine patrol), Tricia avoided eye contact by staring down into her Evian. As it turned out, she was asked to dance despite herself—but she was the first to return to the table.

As I explained to Tricia later, there are energetic, enthusiastic people who are totally unabashed about their zest for life. These men and women don't have to write their phone numbers in telephone booths. It is as though their gestures, their movements, their entire manner proclaim, "For a good time, see me."

As hard as it is to believe, the Tricia I know is also a funny, exciting person. Yet the statement her body language broadcasts is a very unfunny "Don't see me, don't approach me, and don't even think about talking to me."

Certainly there are good reasons for not using your body as a billboard to blatantly advertise your availability. (Tricia speculated that she developed many of her off-putting mannerisms to stave off "model-chasers." Maybe that's why so many beautiful women complain that men are intimidated by them.) Still, the key to being approached is seeming approachable. If you're not issuing any invitations, you aren't likely to get any, either.

THE BODY LANGUAGE OF LOVE

Gregor was a dashing Russian whose parents had emigrated to Brooklyn while he was still a boy. Because of his heavy accent, Gregor was reluctant to engage women in impromptu conversation for fear that they wouldn't understand him. It was a flirting hurdle the class believed Gregor would never overcome, until one warm September night.

"I did it! I went to a concert in the park and talked to a beautiful girl!" he announced with pride. "I even made a date to take her for *rogaliki* in my neighborhood!"

I congratulated Gregor and pressed him for a brief description of *rogaliki*. (They are cresent-shaped walnut pastries.) Then I asked the question the entire class was dying to know.

"There must have been a lot of girls at that concert," I said. "How did you ever decide to speak to that particular one?"

"American girls walk and talk so quickly. I never felt that they would take the time to understand me," he explained. "Nancy was different. She came alone, but she seemed relaxed. She didn't glare at everyone who stepped on the blanket she brought to sit on. And she didn't guard her picnic basket as though someone would steal it." Gregor shrugged. "I felt that if she was that comfortable with herself, she would be comfortable with me."

You know me. I pass out hellos faster than streetcorner evangelists can hand out brochures. And I have advised you to do the same. But as much as I love to flirt with everyone I meet, I know that I am instinctively attracted to men who exude a friendly openness. And so are the adventurous single men and women who are thinking about approaching you.

What do strangers see when they look at you? One thing is certain: they don't see a blank slate. From the top of your head to the tips of your toes, everything you wear and every movement you make telegraphs something about your sense of yourself and your relationship to the world.

Maybe you, like Tricia, are feeling like the third wheel (or spare tire!) of the crowd. Maybe you're simply wondering whether your image is a true reflection of your attitude, emotions, and desires. Whatever your reason, this checklist can help you decide whether your body language attracts or repels others. For a quick, self-administered body language checkup, simply tick off the areas where you think you need improvement. For a more in-depth study, photocopy the list for a friend, fill this one out yourself, then compare notes. Image is in the eye of the beholder. You may need an honest friend to tell you whether the messages you're sending are the ultimate turn-on or an unwitting turn-off.

☐ *The Hair.* Commercials may be full of hot air, but those that feature lustrous, windblown hair are known moneymakers. Why? Hair that moves is touchable—and anything touchable is sexy!

If you're sporting a heavily sprayed helmet of hair, or a comb-over to cover your receding hairline, the message you are sending is, "I am very uptight. Keep hands off."

☐ *The Eyes.* In poll after poll, singles rate the eyes as one of the features they look at first when scoping out the opposite sex. And that technique is right on! Eyes reflect our feelings toward others. Need proof? Take note of the fuzzy "I-don't-see-you" focus we adopt to control our response to a homeless person. Now recall the last time you caught someone staring at you. How did you feel? Frightened? Awkward? As if you were a piece of meat?

As I have said before, staring is no compliment. It is invasive and threatening. And although a glance can be provocative (especially when accompanied by a smile), furtive, sideways looks come across as shifty. (Good flirts may be mysterious but they are never sneaky!) If you look closely, pupils dilate and skin flushes during sexual attraction or arousal. Maybe that's why many of our sexual icons have been blue-eyed with fair skin. Their excitement is a dead giveaway. Being admired and desired are strong aphrodisiacs.

Finally, here's a special note for those of you who wear sunglasses at night or indoors: the message you are sending is, "I can see you but you can't see me." You may be playing at hide-and-seek but you make it seem like a dangerous game.

□ *The nose*. Several kinesiologists have noted that our nostrils flare naturally when we're talking to someone we like. Of course, that's more likely to happen if you don't seem to be looking down your nose at others.

□ *The lips*. Remember the wartime slogan "Loose lips sink ships"? Tight, tense, compressed lips sink relationships, right from the first meeting. The mouth is a gateway in a very real sense, for our emotions, thoughts, and words as well as food. Drawn lips, clenched teeth, and a stiff jaw tell others that we would prefer that gateway to stay shut.

Just as a full, smiling mouth is equated with sensuality, clamped lips speak of a withholding, unemotional nature. They also suggest inner tension, and tension is more contagious than this year's flu. Those who don't want to expose themselves to your stress are sure to shy away.

□ *The shoulders*. Everybody knows what I mean by the cold shoulder, but the hunched shoulder, shrugged shoulder, limp shoulder, and stiff shoulder can give the people you meet an equally chilly feeling.

Fred, a widower at fifty-nine, had had back problems for years. That and a total refusal to do the exercises his physician recommended had given his shoulders a hunched appearance. Fred didn't think much about it until one night in seminar when I asked the group to "freeze" into their positions so that we could study each other's natural body language.

"Fred, you look like you're carrying the weight of the world on your shoulders," commented Carey, a student at a nearby university.

"I've got two kids your age in college, so that's just the way I feel," Fred retorted angrily.

The class retreated immediately. And I couldn't help thinking that most of the women Fred met beat a hasty retreat, too. Whether Fred's posture was the result of an injury or a physical manifestation of stress, his bent, burdened appearance made him seem beaten, as though he was overwhelmed by life. Only a very special woman would offer to take on a man in that condition. Even if she appeared, she would likely be frightened away by Fred's underlying hostility.

But if hunched shoulders convey a sense of oppression, other postures communicate just the opposite. Countless men and women keep their shoulders rolled forward in what looks like a permanent shrug. Their message is, "I don't know and I don't care." And that doesn't give the people they meet much reason to care about them. Still other singles allow their shoulders to hang limp or take on a sloping appearance. The helpless, apathetic feeling that conveys is as unappealing in a woman as it is in a man.

☐ *Posture.* Remember Tricia, the model whose professional poise was poisoning her social life? Well, there was another habit she carried off the runway and into the clubs: ramrod-straight posture. Although a straight, stiff spine is every mother's dream, the wall-like, unyielding image it imparts can be a nightmare to a prospective companion.

Of course, that doesn't mean you should counter a good posture by going into an all-out slump. A slouching, sagging stance connotes boredom, laziness, and spinelessness—and those attributes aren't likely to make anyone stand up and take notice.

☐ *Packaging.* It's unfair but true—singles judge you in the first five minutes after meeting you. So always look your best. Follow simple rules. If you are heavy, wear vertical—never horizontal—stripes. If you are short, try wearing all one color; don't divide yourself too many times. There are courses you can take in image and beauty. It may sound superficial, but being attractive is an asset, and "you never get a second chance to make a first impression."

PERSONAL SPACE IS PERSONAL

Does she or doesn't she . . . want you to come closer, that is? For most of us, it isn't easy to know.

Flirting is a process through which we explore increasing levels of intimacy. At first, you engage another person with your eyes, from across the room. When your interest is acknowledged, perhaps with a smile or a gesture, you are permitted to come closer and begin a conversation. But how close is too close for a first encounter? What are the signals that let you know that you are getting too close for your partner's comfort?

"How close you should get depends on how intimate you want to become," claims Donald, a man who seems to have no problem attracting women.

You may know someone like Donald. While he's a reasonably attractive man, he's not gorgeous. Still, he can move into a room, spot a woman he finds interesting, and know immediately whether she is equally taken by him. When I asked him to explain how he does it, he answered in terms of space. "Everyone has his or her own personal space," he said. "If a woman makes gestures that invite me into her space, I know she's interested."

And what kind of gestures are they? "First of all, she turns her body slightly toward me. That lets me know that she's positively inclined. She may also tilt her head in my direction as if she's hanging on my every word.

"If she's sitting, she might cross her legs in my direction. Or if she's really feeling comfortable with my proximity, she'll uncross them and part them slightly."

And the clincher? Donald smiled knowingly. "That's when she leans forward in my direction or actually reaches for something that's in my personal space. Then I know we've connected."

Women observe similar space issues with men. Remember Barbara from Chapter 3, the effervescent woman in her thirties? She told me about a man she noticed across the room at a large wedding reception. "He kept looking at me, just long enough to catch my gaze. He'd smooth his pants, or straighten his tie, then glance up again to see if I was still watching.

"After a few of those pants/tie moves, when he was sure he had my interest, he leaned in my direction, nodded, and rested his hand on his knee. I took this to mean it was okay to enter his space and I walked over. The closer I came, the more he turned his body toward mine until I was directly in front of him. At that point, he crossed his arms over his chest, so I knew he didn't want me to come any closer. We chatted for a few minutes and, when the conversation seemed to be going in the right direction, he uncrossed his arms and indicated that I should sit with him.

"Once we were across the table from each other, my new friend really turned on the expressions of interest. He lowered his conversational tone to pull me further into his personal space. Several times, he reached toward me, resting his hands on my side of the table. Finally, when we found that we had many interests in common, he took a glass of champagne from a waiter and set it a few inches from me. That told me that he was taking care of me, that he found me to be more special than the other guests. And that's the kind of message you don't have to be a code-breaker to decipher!"

Nevertheless, Barbara is quite a code-breaker. Now a successful novelist, she used her acute powers of observation and her knowledge of human behavior to decode many of the common nonverbal signals that let us know it's okay to get up close and personal with the people we meet. She recognized her acquaintance's tie-straightening for what it was: preening behavior. And whether it's an ostrich fluffing its feathers or a woman smoothing her hair, that kind of gesture always means, "I want to look good for you."

Barbara was also correct in assuming that her new friend's crossed arms meant that she was getting too close. Experts say we often display unconscious signals when our space is being invaded and we're not ready for it. (When a man I hardly knew once pulled the chair I was sitting on close to his, I reacted instinctively by thrusting my arms out and pushing him away.) Barbara's willingness to defer to her new friend's ambivalence—and her good sense not to get in his face—let him know that she wanted to share his space, not overrun it. That's what ultimately made him feel more positive about her.

Allowing someone to enter your space is a very personal thing. After all, your movements are speaking an extremely intimate language. When your body language is saying, "I am interested in you; I'd like to get to know you better," you're making a courageous admission.

Choosing to enter another's personal space is also a statement of interest and an act of bravery. By doing so, you confront your fear that you have misread someone else's signals, your rejection anxiety, and your attraction to a person who is still a virtual stranger.

However, getting closer to someone doesn't have to be an all-or-nothing, sink-or-swim proposition. There are ways of testing the water—and the limits of your partner's comfort zone—before you leap in with both feet. You could, for instance, reach toward your conversational partner (without actually touching!) to gesture to an object of interest nearby. If he or she pulls back or reacts strongly, you know the relationship is strictly hands-off for now. If you are at a restaurant or seated at a bar, you might begin to place a few of your personal objects—like your wine glass, your purse, or a book—on your acquaintance's side of the table.

If he or she allows the "invasion," it's a sure sign that you are welcome to increase the intimacy.

I can't guarantee that your overtures will always be met with open arms. (Some flirts are married, you know!) But body language doesn't lie. If you give the object of your flirtation enough space—generally an arm's length—he or she will let you know when it's time to close the gap.

TOUCH IS A TOUCHY SUBJECT

Alex and Susan were having an exciting conversation about their mutual love of horses when Bernie, a friend of Alan's, walked over. In a burst of enthusiasm, Alan threw his arm over Susan's shoulder and said, "Bernie, meet my new friend, Susan. With any luck, she'll be riding with me next week!"

Susan immediately tensed, mumbled something about having to find the girlfriend she had come with, and ran off. Alan was puzzled. What had he done wrong?

His most obvious mistake was not waiting for a signal from Susan that permission to touch her had been granted. True, his spontaneous embrace was a platonic one. The brief arm-around-the-shoulder-clench is a harmless hold—and one we see every week among players on Monday Night Football. Still, the shock of being touched at all, teamed as it was with the "riding" comment (which Susan construed as a double entendre) made Susan feel sexually threatened. To her, it didn't feel like flirting—it felt like an invasion.

Why does touch strike a nerve with so many of us? Because being touched in the here and now recalls the ways we were touched as children. If you grew up in a warm, "huggy" home where caresses and embraces were given out as regularly as cookies and juice, your recommended daily allowance of touch is probably on the high side. You may have a problem keeping your hands off people you

like—or you may have learned by experience to reserve
those "touchy-feelies" for the people you really love. If, on
the other hand, your family was not so effusive, you may
experience casual touching as confusing, off-putting, or too
familiar.

Cultural issues aside, women are, on the whole, more
sensitive and private about touch. They resent being fon-
dled like inanimate sex objects. And no matter who was
most instrumental in teaching them the importance of self-
respect—their mothers, their fathers, their religious in-
structors, or Gloria Steinem—the men they are looking for
are those who will respect their wishes about the touchy
subject of touch. A woman I met recently, who happened to
be a lapsed member of a conservative religion, summed it
up this way: "As a kid I learned that my body was a temple
of the Holy Spirit. Now I think my body is a temple for *my*
spirit. So I told this guy I was dancing with, 'My hips are
not handles. If you really need something to hold on to,
maybe you shouldn't be dancing at all!' "

So where is it okay to touch? The rules change with increasing intimacy, but on first meeting the rule is hard and
fast: it's strictly hands-off except for the area between the
fingertips and the elbows.

SHAKE IT UP

Mark, a burly sports fanatic in my seminar, identified himself early on as a Terminator Flirt. His reaction to the
fingertip-elbow rule made me suspect that his physical aggression with women was what caused most of his relationships to terminate.

"You mean, I can touch her hands, but that's it?" he
choked.

"That's it," I answered.

"Wow ... dating without groping," he sighed. "What's

the next lesson? No kissing until the engagement? No sex until marriage?"

Touch—especially that first physical connection between people who are attracted to each other—is an extremely powerful communicator. True, a handshake may not be as intensely intimate as a kiss, but there is nothing like that first finger-to-finger contact with an exciting new prospect to send an electric feeling coursing up our arms. Why? Because even the most socially acceptable forms of touch put people within reach of each other's largest, most sensitive sexual organ: their skin. And because the skin is a veritable hotbed of highly responsive nerve endings, the merest brush, stroke, or caress is all that's needed to send a *very* stimulating message.

GIVING YOURSELF A FAIR SHAKE

Like all our conscious and unconscious gestures, a handshake can communicate something about our personalities—or a persona we wish to convey. A firm handshake, for example, is a business mainstay because it sends a strong, self-confident message. An assured grip announces to the world, "I'm good at what I do. You can count on me."

There are also handshakes that convey an underlying sense of insecurity. A bone-crushing clasp, for example, speaks of a desire to overwhelm but an inability to do so in a socially acceptable way. It says, "I can't bowl you over with my personality, so I'll make an impression with brute force." (And if you've ever gotten a handshake like that while you were wearing rings, it undoubtedly did make an impression!)

At one time or another, we've all been on the receiving end of a limp, dead-fish handshake—and as much as we didn't like the lifeless feeling of the grip, we probably liked the message we got even less. What does this straight-from-the-mortuary clasp communicate? "I'm obligated to shake your hand, but really, I'd rather not touch you," or "I'm not very secure and confident. Are you sure you want to get to know me?"

So what's the best technique for a sexy, seductive shake? Among the men and women in my seminars, the hand-over-hand clasp wins hands down. Men say that when a woman offers her hand, then covers the grip with her other hand, it makes them feel important and liked. Willem described the effect this way: "Any two people can shake hands. But when a woman surrounds my hand with hers, she lets me know that she is taking the encounter very personally. I know that if I ask her out, she's sure to say yes." And the feeling is mutual for women. They say that the hand-over-hand shake leaves them feeling secure, cared for, and attractive. And a woman can always find something attractive about a man who is obviously attracted to her!

Of course, it's possible that this kind of suave, almost Continental interdigitation might seem a little too Cary Grant for your jeans-and-T-shirt persona. No problem. The next time you're out and about on the party circuit and you find someone who is more attractive to you than the hors d'oeuvres, just give your regular shake a personal touch. Hold your acquaintance's hand a second or two longer than you normally would. Then look directly into his or her eyes and say, "It was a pleasure to meet you." Or just brush your partner's hand with yours. It only takes a light touch to get your message through loud and clear.

ARE YOU AN "ACTIVE" LISTENER?

If you learn more about a person by using your ears instead of your mouth, then you probably are taking advantage of some "active" listening techniques. But if listening is the part of the communication process that you normally don't work at, or if you think of your ears as a convenient place to hang your sunglasses, you are not making the most of your auditory sense. And that's a big mistake if effective flirting is your goal.

What is active listening? It is a specific set of techniques based on the belief that receiving information is as important to the communication process as giving information. Hailed from its inception as a breakthrough therapeutic and social technique, active listening is the ultimate win-win situation. Its goal is twofold: first, to make others feel cared for, listened to, understood, and appreciated, and second, to turn you into a more empathetic, tuned-in listener.

Active listening is a subtle, simple skill, yet its results can truly transform the way you flirt, date, and relate. Because it requires you to give regard and respect to others, it is a nonthreatening way to gather information. And because active listening makes others feel comfortable in your presence, it encourages them to open up to you. They reveal the way they feel and think without ever being asked. And that enables *you* to decide whether to put them into your little black book in pencil, in pen, or not at all.

Of course, there's more to active listening than can be covered in this brief chapter. (It is, after all, a therapeutic device, and the subject of many professional books.) Still, I'm satisfied that the basic strategies I've outlined here will enhance your social skills, expand your conversational options, and help you get the most informational mileage out of every second you spend flirting. That's precisely what they did for a compulsive talker I know named Susan.

OH, THOSE IRRESISTIBLE EARS!

On first meeting Susan, I just knew she had been a cheerleader in college. Petite, bubbly, and full of boundless energy, Susan not only had the spirit, but she made sure that everybody got a chance to hear it. From the seminar participants to passersby on the streets, she regaled the world with stories about her quaint hometown (population 879), the tale of how she found her great rent-controlled apartment (the super was a fellow alum), or the epic about how she got that "hideous scar on her knee" (collision with a balance beam). In fact, there was only one thing Susan didn't talk about very much: repeat dates. That was because she didn't get many.

The men Susan preferred were quite unlike her. Because she went for the strong, burly, earthy type in a big way, Peter was not a man she would have chosen for herself. Nevertheless, Susan's best friend, Janice, thought Peter was just the ticket for her unlucky buddy—and she arranged a blind date for a Saturday night.

As it turned out, Peter was a very important man in the company where Janice worked. How did Susan discover that he was important? He told her so all night long! Peter had a big car, a big job, a big cigar, and a tremendous ego. And although Susan was bored to tears by Peter's bragging, she endured the ordeal like a trooper—until it came time to order dessert.

Perhaps it was an innocent selection. Perhaps it was an unconscious reflection of Susan's wish to deep-six this date. But when the waiter handed her the menu, she knew just what she wanted: "Death by Chocolate."

"Are you kidding?" Peter snapped. "That dessert is deadly! It's loaded with sugar—and what isn't sugar is fat! I consider my body to be a temple. I would never desecrate it with such junk."

Susan, for perhaps the first time in her life, was speechless. This man had already killed off an entire evening. Now he was ruining the only moment of pleasure she had managed to salvage. Unable to voice her anger, she clammed up totally—leaving Peter to fill the void between them with the sound of his own voice.

Susan's distaste for this boorish braggart was obvious to her, but apparently not to Peter. When dinner was over, he invited her to his apartment to share his favorite noncaloric nightcap: Perrier. When she turned him down and headed to the curb to hail a cab, he took her arm—and surprised her again. "I've had such a wonderful evening," he crooned. "I think you're such an interesting person. Can't we see each other again soon? How about next Saturday night? I have two tickets to the Philharmonic."

Susan didn't know what to say. She loved Lincoln Center—but hated the thought of enduring another of Peter's Me, Myself, and I marathons. Still, she told herself, first impressions can be misleading. She agreed to go—and began regretting her decision as soon as the word "yes" had passed her lips.

Unfortunately, Susan's regret was not unfounded. If anything, Peter was even louder and prouder than the week before. Susan spent the evening nodding dazedly at his self-important opinions and self-centered anecdotes, and uh-huhing at all the questions he asked her—and answered himself. But when Peter complimented her on her listening skills, Susan's curiosity was piqued. And when he capped the dismal evening by asking her out on a third date, the reason for his interest became abundantly clear: he didn't want to hear a woman talk; he wanted to hear a woman listen! To Peter, it simply didn't matter whether Susan's drowsy nods and stupefied grunts helped her stay awake through the tedium of his company. He *believed* she was listening—and that validated Peter in a way he had never been validated before.

This is a real, true-life story—and it has several very real morals. It demonstrates how insensitive people can be when they don't listen at all. (Susan finally did break the relationship off for precisely that reason.) But it also shows the value of being a great listener! All her life, Susan had bubbled, babbled, and enthused to keep the men around her entertained, and she never got anything to show for it but the dubious title "Queen of the First Dates." Once she shut her mouth and let someone else do the talking, Susan became the object of hot pursuit by Peter as well as several other suitors.

But there is one more moral to Susan's saga, and that is that no story ever really ends. Susan became so engrossed by what she had learned from her experience with Peter that she began to study the subtle art of listening both academically and socially. One day in school, she learned what her instructor called the "echo technique"—a verbal mirroring skill in which you repeat the speaker's message without judgment or criticism. That night she began to use it in conversation, to open others up and invite deeper discourse. Later she was introduced to the more sophisticated "third ear" technique, which enabled her to seek out the underlying needs and feelings of others. Shortly thereafter, she began to notice that friends, relatives, and attractive men sought her company more often than ever.

Susan is still single by choice. In fact, she says it'd be a crime for her to marry now that she's learned to parlay a handful of words into an abundance of great dates. But of all the techniques she has learned, Susan pinpoints one listening method as the secret behind her success with the opposite sex. That powerful strategy is called the Three R's.

THE THREE R'S

Readin', 'ritin', and 'rithmetic may be *the* three R's to know if you're balancing your checkbook, but if you're juggling an uneven conversation the key is to *Repeat* your partner's words to him or her, *Rephrase* each statement as it comes, and *Reflect* the attention on your conversational partner.

The Three R's technique works particularly well for the fledgling flirt not only because it is easy to use, but because it is an all-purpose, foolproof method. By simply repeating and rephrasing a conversational partner's words,

you can validate the speaker, make him or her want to elu-
cidate further, diffuse anger, and steer the course of the
conversation to much greater depth. And by constantly reflecting the focus of the discourse away from you, you encourage an acquaintance to reveal more and more of
himself or herself, allowing you to glimpse the underlying
needs and emotions behind his or her opinions.

For a look at how the Three R's can rescript a conversation, I need only recall one chat I had at a holiday party
not long ago.

As soon as I got my foot in the door, I could see that
this party had a Noah's Ark theme. Everyone seemed to
have come with a partner—that is, everyone except me and
Troy, a man I had met once before at the host's country
home. I hung up my coat, greeted some of the other guests,
then made my way across the room where, in lieu of a
girlfriend, Troy was making some pretty heavy contact
with the punch bowl.

"I know you, don't I?" he demanded. "And if I don't, do
I want to?"

"I—I don't know . . ." I stammered, completely taken
aback by the unexpected confrontation. "I mean, yes, we've
met."

Troy topped off his cup. "Then tell me one thing. Are
you full of the holiday spirit? Because if you are, I'd appreciate it if you'd go ho-ho-ho somebody else. I'm just not in
the mood."

By then, neither was I. I had come to the party brim-
ming with good cheer. The last thing I needed was an encounter with a curmudgeonly man who wanted to play
Scrooge to my Bob Cratchit. My first impulse was to empty
the punch bowl into his pants. Instead, I poured myself a
cup and, not knowing what else to say, rephrased his challenge for him. "You mean you're not in the mood for a
party?"

Troy shook his head. "Actually, I'm not in the mood for

holidays," he answered, this time in a softer tone of voice. "See, Santa already visited me—and he dumped a great big load of coal right into my stocking. So my holidays have gone up in smoke, so to speak."

I know what you're thinking. I'm the one who told you to excuse yourself as quickly as possible from dead-end conversations like this one. But by now, I was intrigued. The trait I had found so enjoyable in Troy during our first meeting was his self-deprecating sense of humor. I was relieved to see that it had not been thrown away along with last year's Christmas tree. Still, I couldn't help wondering what had gone so awry in his recent life. Keeping the focus clearly on Troy, I reflected his statement at him one more time.

"So, Santa really unloaded on you, did he?"

"He did," Troy nodded. "But the old coward didn't even have the guts to do the dirty deed himself. He sent my ex-wife's lawyer as a stand-in. He not only gave me a summons I didn't ask for, he didn't even bother to have it gift-wrapped!"

By now, Troy was concentrating more on his feelings and less on the punch bowl—and since I had gotten to the root of his problem, we could converse on a subject we had in common: the trials and tribulations of divorce. By simply reiterating each of his statements, I gave Troy the sense that it was okay to feel bad—even during a festive season. What followed next was the kind of in-depth conversation that turns relatively new acquaintances into old pals—and a mutual feeling of deepening friendship that gave us both a reason to celebrate.

Of course, you don't have to agree with everything a date or conversational partner says in order to validate him or her. (Yes-men and -women are too wishy-washy to be really good flirts!) Validation simply means accepting another person's point of view as real—and that requires no compromise of your conflicting opinions.

All it really takes to make someone feel accepted is to show you've been listening. By repeating, rephrasing, and reflecting another person's words, what you are really saying is, "I may not agree with you, but I've heard you." And in this acceptance-starved world, that's usually all the encouragement it takes to help a new friend open up.

THE SILENT TREATMENT

I asked a good friend of mine to take a look at the first draft of this book. When she got to this headline, she burst out laughing. "Are you sure you mean silent *treatment?*" she asked me. "I think of silence as torture!"

Silence certainly can be a form of torture, particularly when it is symbolic of another, more disturbing, kind of withholding. But a treatment is a remedy by definition. And in the hands of a skilled active listener, silence can be just the cure for a reticent companion.

For one thing, a certain amount of silence allows the speaker to be alone with his thoughts, to sort them out, and to focus on what's most important to him. Allowing the speaker that time to quietly compose himself will make him feel more comfortable with you. (Need proof? Think back to the last time you were pressured to respond to a highly charged question or felt badgered. How do you feel now about your answer? About the person who forced you to answer?)

Once your companion begins to trust you—and the silence—continued quiet can then act as a gentle prod, nudging him toward deeper disclosure.

Of course, too much of a good thing can be, well . . . too much. If your eyes start to take on a zombie-like stare or if you notice your companion drumming her fingers on the table, it's time to liven things up a bit. Remember: effective silence is active; unproductive silence is just plain monotonous.

DON'T JUST SIT THERE—SAY SOMETHING!

Your body language and listening skills can be your greatest assets or biggest bugaboos. Use these exercises to become more conscious of the nonverbal signals you're sending and others are sure to become more conscious of you!

A PICTURE IS WORTH A THOUSAND WORDS

. . . especially when your body language is the subject. Just don't expect still photographs to give you an accurate picture of the face you use to greet the world. Pictures do lie when they're posed. And that happy smile that comes so naturally to you when you're among friends may not be so warm and welcoming when you're out among strangers.

For a true image of your image, go to the videotape! Ask your uncle (the one who has not seen a family event except through the lens of his camcorder!) for that tape he made of Cousin Enid's graduation party. Better yet, ask to view a professionally made videotape of a recent wedding or party where you may have been caught unaware. What do you see? If you are the daunting poker face at the table, then you need to break in some smile lines. Is your posture stiff and uninviting? Loosen up! That ramrod-straight back makes you look as inflexible and unreachable as a telephone pole.

ARE YOU LISTENING?

To find out, practice listening with a partner at home. Pick a subject and let your friend talk about it without interruption for five minutes while you concentrate on what she is saying. Then echo her message back to her. Did you get it right? Did she feel understood, appreciated, validated? Or just the opposite—judged, challenged, threatened, or ignored? If the latter, you didn't get her message. And the people you meet are probably trying to tell you something. Catch yourself in the future and listen actively. Successful friendships will surely follow.

A QUIET REMINDER

Remember:

- Don't act on a single verbal cue. It's like RSVP'ing to a party before you've been invited. Wait for a cluster of messages.
- Be aware of your own body language. Others are.
- Personal space is personal. Don't invade.
- Touch is a powerful communicator. Use it sparingly.
- A handshake instead of a kiss? Why not? It can be just as seductive.
- Talking too much is a sure sign that you aren't listening.
- Use the Three R's: Repeat, Rephrase, and Reflect.
- You can learn more in a minute of silence than you can in hours of mindless conversation.
- Don't confront. Validate!
- Listening is an active process. If you're not working at it, it's not working for you.

6

HEARING AND HANDLING THE *N* WORD

"I talked to her for nearly ten minutes. Then I asked her if she wanted to go for coffee. Now all I remember of the conversation is that she said no." —DAVID, age 38

"No!" In the first year of our lives, it's the most powerful word we learn to speak. In all the years that follow, it's a word we learn to fear, deny, or resent. And how could it be otherwise? As babies it was the word that stood between us and what we thought of as autonomy. As teenagers, it was the wet blanket our dates—and our parents—threw over our raging hormones. What we ended up grasping from those encounters was the idea that a simple two-letter word could keep us from true love, true lust, or even curiosity.

As adults, we still hear the *N* word more often than we

would like. In fact, our opportunities for rejection (and many of them *are* opportunities!) seem to grow with us, touching not only our social lives but our careers, our dealings with friends, and our family relationships. And as our chances of rejection grow, so do our feelings *about* rejection. It's as if, somewhere between two and twenty, we lose our sense of healthy resentment along with our baby fat. And because so many of us replace it with self-blame, feelings of inadequacy, and negative thinking, adults—especially single adults—no longer have to hear the "no" to feel its effect. The anticipation of rejection is enough to stop us in our tracks, to keep us from reaching out, to limit our chances for successful flirting.

Michael, a divorced man in one of my seminars, was a case in point. At age forty-two, he had recently landed a top job as the director of publicity for a large publishing company. With his kindly good looks and gentle, open manner, he had everything he needed to make him successful at meeting women, too. So when he confessed that he had not been out on "a real date" in more than two years, the group—especially the female contingent—tuned in fast.

Marcia, a no-holds-barred personality, was the first to speak. "What do you mean you haven't been out on any *real* dates?" she challenged. "What have these encounters been? *Un*real?"

"Sort of," Michael answered. "I go to parties. I go out for drinks with women friends. I do lunch. I just tend to do those things with a group rather than one woman at a time."

"So you are meeting women," I commented. "And I assume that some of them have been interesting to you. Why haven't you asked to see any of them individually?"

Michael shrugged. "I'm just not the aggressive type."

"But you were aggressive enough to go after the job you wanted," Marcia said. "Even after being laid off for six months."

"I was laid off because of cutbacks," Michael said defensively. "You can't take cutbacks personally. But getting cut out of somebody's life? That hits where it really hurts."

As Michael saw it, he had two choices. He could enroll in the school of hard knocks, go for some one-to-one contact, and risk an occasional rejection. Or he could beat the no to the punch and reject himself rather than let any potential date make that decision for him.

But there was another option that Michael had not considered. As Marcia pointed out, Michael had been laid off at the height of his career. Certainly he could have taken his pink slip personally. For most of us, being "cut back" is the ultimate professional no. But Michael didn't let that rejection stop him. And he didn't let himself become one of a crowd, even in a market teeming with job-hunters. Instead, he let his individual talents shine, made his goals known, and successfully turned a rejection into an opportunity. Can't a man who is assertive enough to pursue the job of his dreams use the same positive philosophy to pursue what might be the relationship of a lifetime? Can't we all?

The truth is we can change our lives if we change our thinking. If you don't want to be alone, if you are tired of wasting time and energy on fearing, denying, or anticipating the rejections we all inevitably face, it's time to begin thinking of the N word in more positive terms. No may be a brush-off, but it can sweep us on to bigger and better things—like the opportunity to understand what rejection really is . . . and what it isn't. Here are some truths about rejections.

#1: REJECTION IS NOT PERSONAL.

One hot summer evening at a singles party, I decided it was time that I became a fully liberated woman. Instead of waiting around at my table hoping that the "right" man would ask me to dance, I would select Mr. Right myself, let him know that it takes two to tango, then sweep him onto the dance floor like Ginger Rogers.

It didn't take me long to find a potential partner: an interesting-looking man had just taken a seat at the bar. I got to my feet, put on my friendliest smile, and asked him if he would like to join me for a dance.

He didn't equivocate. He didn't hesitate. He looked me square in the eye and said, "No."

It seemed to me that the DJ had suddenly taken a break and everyone in the place had taken a vow of silence. It wasn't just a no, it was the no heard around the world. And you know the cliché about wishing the floor would open and swallow you whole? Well, I actually looked down at my feet, hoping.

Then I began to follow my own advice. I got back on my "flirting horse" and marched on to the next guy who seemed appealing. The next thing I knew, I had a dance partner—and a new friend.

Later that evening, my first choice made his way over to me at the buffet table. "I wanted to explain," he began. "It wasn't that I didn't want to dance with you. I was just getting over a long, miserable trip on the expressway. I was hot, tired, and more than a little cranky. All I really wanted to do was sit awhile and relax."

Maybe it's because we're all so conscious of our imperfections that we think they're perfectly obvious to everyone else. Or maybe we tend to blame ourselves simply because we are the most convenient targets. But we are all so busy taking rejection personally that we never stop to think about all the impersonal reasons there are to say no.

Okay, so the man of my dreams turned out to be the Master Flirt's nightmare. But he didn't turn me down because I was too short in stature or too long on assertion. And he didn't give me the brush because my lipstick was smudged, my stockings were wrinkled, or my voice was too shrill. In fact, he didn't reject *me* at all. All he rejected was the opportunity to dance. This story helped me to develop a philosophy of rejection. We all need one.

Think back on the last time a flirting encounter ended

with you rerunning that worn-out tape of your shortcomings. Is it possible that you reminded him of his mother—or didn't remind him of his mother? Could she simply have preferred the Wall Street type? The Bohemian artist type? The intellectual-with-thick-glasses type? If so, then maybe, just maybe you need to view refusal in a different light.

#2: REJECTION IS A FAVOR.

I call him Adonis Atadistance. You can call him or her by name. How do I know that you can supply a name? Because we have all, at one time or another, glimpsed a person who—at a distance—seemed to be the ultimate perfection of his or her gender and the total fulfillment of our wildest sexual imaginings. Of course, few of us could imagine actually approaching such a person. (We were only fledgling flirts then.) So instead, we pined, we longed ... we imagined worshiping that person physically in ways that are humanly impossible. And then the worst possible thing happened. We met.

As it turned out, my Adonis Atadistance was a self-consumed cad who couldn't put three words together in his native language. When he bid me adieu, he used only two: "Get lost."

Was I devastated? At first. It isn't easy saying goodbye to a fantasy—and that's just what most of his attractive characteristics turned out to be. But a few months later, I could see that Adonis had actually done me a far bigger favor by leaving me than he ever would have done by loving me. My image of him was clearly overinflated—like a balloon. When he stuck a pin in it (by sticking it to me!), he set me free to find a kinder, gentler, smarter man. And that's just what I did.

To some extent, we all see what we want to see, both in ourselves and in others. That's why so many of the promising people we meet turn out to be "nothing like what we thought they were" after the first date.

In retrospect, it really doesn't matter why my Adonis rejected me. He may have been threatened by my ability to answer a question with something other than a grunt. He might have been concerned that dating one girl at a time might ruin his reputation as a ladies' man—or take too much time away from his bodybuilding program. Whatever the reason, he didn't reject *me* because he never got to know me. And more important, he didn't monopolize my time. He did me the favor of turning me loose quickly, giving me a chance to get on with my life—and the fun of flirting.

The lesson here is obvious: immediate turn-downs are never setbacks. They're opportunities to move forward! Sure, rejection stings—especially at point-blank range. But the stranger who gives you the brush quickly isn't going to turn into a Nowhere Man. (You know the guy: he wastes three months of your life, then tells you that the relationship is going nowhere.) With a positive philosophy of rejection, you simply won't have time to obsess over the one that got away. You'll be too busy filling your little black book with the phone numbers of more compatible new friends.

#3: TURNING REJECTION AROUND.

No one can be a mind reader and yet we all try so hard to figure out why someone has rejected us. Since we have no foolproof way of knowing *why* someone has rejected us, I suggest you develop a *philosophy of rejection* that will help you continue to be active in the dating world. In so doing, I suggest defense mechanisms, psychological behaviors such as rationalization (making an excuse) and projection (throwing the blame onto another), to make the *N* word more palatable and help you not to dwell on the negative. Psychologists may consider it unhealthy to employ these defenses, and if you used them all the time with everyone and everything, I would have to agree. But in the difficult singles scene, I want you to be spared pain and to make sure you continue flirting. So let's try these techniques. (The only exception is if you are *always* getting rejected, then you must examine the reasons. Ask a friend what you are doing wrong, or see a therapist for awareness and improvement. Sometimes it's as simple as what you are wearing, sloppy habits, interrupting others' conversations, or talking too loudly. But for most of us, I give permission to make excuses and throw the blame on others for rejecting you without ever really knowing you.)

Think of it this way: maybe you remind him of his ex and she won't let him see the kids, or her ex who is two years late with the support check. Or you remind him of the gal who broke his heart, borrowed his credit cards and plunged him into bankruptcy. Or maybe he likes tall, thin, leggy model types and you are short, smart, and pleasingly plump. Have you ever considered her preference for hiking, camping, and outdoorsmen and your awful allergy to trees that makes you love an indoor fireplace and chaise?

I say it's not your fault if he or she rejected you. This person does not have good taste and certainly is not aware of your great inner qualities. Make an excuse, any excuse, and move on. Who are they rejecting anyway? They don't know you. He doesn't understand quick-witted women; she's so serious, and he likes his women with a sense of humor and a frequent giggle. Throwing the blame works equally as well as excuse making. We can't make it together because he doesn't understand when I describe my job in biological research; he hates women who wear large glasses; she dislikes vests and red power ties. Anything that works for you and prevents you from taking the *N* word seriously is legitimate. In the singles game, use all the equipment you can to help you play, and if that means inventing excuses why she doesn't laugh at your jokes or he won't disco dance with you, rationalize and project in your most creative ways and set your sights elsewhere.

#4: REJECTION IS NOT SERIOUS.

"Friends? Who's looking for friends?" commented Jessica, a petite brunette I met after a lecture. "I don't need another buddy to shop with. I need somebody special. Somebody I can love."

Don't we all! But as I told Jessica, setting your sights for full-blown romance is like mining only for the Hope Diamond. If you find it, your life will be enriched beyond your dreams. If you don't, your search will become desperate and unhappy. Worst of all, you will have missed all the smaller gems you might have found along the way.

Out of brief encounters, great relationships can grow. And in a million surprising ways! If you find yourself passing up a conversation with Mr. Interesting because he may not be the marrying kind, you are cheating yourself out of the opportunity to meet a man who may be your next boss, or your yoga instructor, or the love of your life. And if you find yourself editing out women who seem "quiet," "modest," or "uptight," you're not flirting—you're hunting! And your sexual intentions are probably more obvious to the women you meet than they are to you.

Remember: the joy of flirting is that it enables you to explore the world of available men and women "without serious intent." If social occasions leave you feeling frustrated or desperate, if you need to check your serious intentions at the party door, try this surefire technique: enter the room, make yourself comfortable, then take a moment to look over the crowd. Without judging, make a quick mental note of three people you find attractive. When the opportunity arises, strike up a conversation with your first choice. If there is a spark, exchange cards or telephone numbers, *then move on to your next prospect.* If during the course of the evening you are rejected or ignored, don't take the rejection personally. Simply shake hands and seek out a more companionable companion.

A man in one of my seminars actually expanded this

technique into what he calls "The Nine-Out-of-Ten Law of Rejection." Truly dedicated to the proposition that singles should go out more and experience rejection less, he actually listed nine no's and one yes on a piece of paper. Then he carried that list with him throughout the week. Each time he heard the *N* word, he crossed out one of the no's and said a silent "Hallelujah!" With that strategy as the basis of his personal philosophy, he was able to get over each unimportant no that came his way, certain that it had brought him just a little bit closer to what might be a very significant yes.

Meeting that special person is now and always has been a numbers game. Even Grandma, who may have warned you about the number of frogs in life's kissing booth, understood that single men and women have to work their way through a lot of no's before getting the right yes. By separating your long-term goals and serious needs from the flirting process, you can successfully separate your innermost self from rejection. Then you'll believe as I do when I say . . .

#5: REJECTION IS NOT THE END OF THE WORLD.

Dr. Albert Ellis is a world-renowned psychologist whose unique approach to psychotherapy has helped millions of people to evaluate and change the destructive thinking that makes them unhappy. He is also a man whose unique approach to rejection can add some perspective to our understanding of the *N* word.

He tells the story that as a shy young man, he wanted to meet some young women. So one day, while strolling through the Bronx Botanical Gardens, he decided it was time to put his irrational fears of rejection behind him. Stationing himself on a park bench in a beautiful location, he set himself this goal: he would go to the park every day during the month of June and ask each and every young woman who happened to sit down beside him for a date.

One by one, women came to rest on the bench. And one by one, Dr. Ellis engaged them in small talk, then popped the question. At the end of the month, the brilliant man who would one day be known as the father of Rational-Emotive Therapy had asked out one hundred women—and gotten ninety-nine no's. Then he found that his one taker had taken him. She never showed up for their rendezvous.

"So what's the moral of this story? That even geniuses get rejected?" asked Ben, a seminar participant and psychology student. "That's not exactly reassuring, is it?"

Or is it? For most of the singles in my workshops, it doesn't hurt to hear that rejection is an equal-opportunity annoyance. Knowing that it affects executives, billionaires, artists, and yes, even renowned psychotherapists does help to take the personal onus off the rest of us. But that's not the moral of the story.

As Dr. Ellis tells it, his one-month rejection blitz taught him two important lessons. First, it isn't absolutely necessary for your mental health and well-being to be loved by everyone you meet, even though it is preferable and definitely the nicer alternative. And second, rejection—even the point-blank, in-your-face kind—is not worth fearing at all. He had imagined the worst, experienced the worst, and lived to tell the tale. And rather than feeling as though his world had ended, he knew that a new era of his life—one free of shyness and fear—had just begun.

"If something like that happened to me, I wouldn't become a psychotherapist. I would become the patient of a psychotherapist!" said Marta, a single friend.

I told her I knew what she meant. Subjecting yourself to other people's whims and desires means making yourself vulnerable to your personal fears and bugaboos. But if you, like Marta, have been socially paralyzed by what you *think* might happen, if you are acting on your own worst-case scenario rather than the appeal of the eligible, attractive people around you, it is time to put an end to that end-of-the-world feeling.

Try this. Imagine yourself in the setting where you last saw—and did not flirt with—a person who interested you. In your mind's eye, see yourself putting on your friendliest smile and making an approach. Now imagine that compelling stranger responding in the worst possible way.

When I tried this exercise with Marta, she immediately recalled a nonencounter she had had with a well-built young man in her local grocery store. "In my imagination, I asked Mr. Tall, Dark, and Couponless something innocuous, like where I could find the peanut butter. He looked at me as though I were crazy and shouted, 'Peanut butter? I can't believe any sane human being actually eats that stuff! Don't you know that peanut butter is full of fat and cholesterol?'

"Here's the worst part," Marta went on. "He looked me up and down and shook his head. Then he said, really disgustedly, 'Peanut butter . . . and you wonder where you got those thunder thighs.' "

I had to hand it to Marta: her imagined encounter had covered all the bases including an insult to her intellect, physical ridicule, and an outright rejection. She never even found out where the peanut butter was! Still, the exercise had had the desired effect. In her fantasy, Marta had experienced the worst that could happen. She allowed herself to feel the pain and humiliation of the moment. But in the end, she was able to laugh about it. "What it took Dr. Ellis one whole day and one hundred rejections to discover, I found out in five minutes!" she gloated.

"And what was that?" I asked, happy that the visualization technique had done its job.

"That nobody ever truly dies from embarrassment. Though you may wish you had, for a moment."

Several months later, Marta was more alive than ever—and happily dating a new man she had met in the library. And what about the phantom of the supermarket? Not only did she see him again, in frozen foods, but she spoke right up. As it turned out, he was a cold fish. She said good-bye and moved on.

HOW TO TAKE NO FOR AN ANSWER

Disappointments, turndowns, and even putdowns are a part of life. But that's no reason to accept negativity as a *way* of life!

These exercises won't form a rejection-proof shield around your ego. (Who wants to meet Robo-Flirt?) But they will help you to maintain your perspective and sanity.

INVENTORY YOUR ASSETS

Make a list of your achievements. Include your talents (you make a great chicken Kiev), your professional successes (perhaps you've been named Salesman of the Year in your division), your skills (what a tennis backhand!), and those personal attributes you like most about yourself (that killer smile). Now put the list in your wallet, or in an appointment book or journal you carry every day where you can read it each time you approach a prospective partner (or reread it after a rejection). Nothing succeeds like success, and you are a success! Just check your list if you don't believe it. It's there in black and white.

GETTING TO YES

On a sheet of paper, list nine no's and one yes. Then each time you hear the *N* word, cross out one of the no's, and remind yourself that you're one step closer to a positive response.

THE TEFLON TECHNIQUE

Self-blame just doesn't stick to the Teflon Flirt! If you're still personalizing each rejection that comes your way, try keeping a rejection log like the one below.

Use the first column to recall your approach; in the second, jot down the negative response. The third column is for positive self-talk. Use this space to list three reasons why that interesting stranger might have rejected your invitation—but not *you.*

I Said:	*S/He Said:*	*Positive Self-Talk:*
I asked a woman in my office if she wanted to get some sushi.	She hates sushi.	1. She really does hate sushi. 2. She doesn't know what sushi is. 3. She's allergic to fish.

READING BETWEEN THE LINES

Meeting an intriguing new person is like beginning a fascinating book. We just can't wait to see what each new chapter will bring. But when an encounter ends in rejection, it feels as though the book has been suddenly slammed shut, leaving behind a multitude of unanswered questions.

Every minute you spend pondering another person's secret thoughts and hidden motives is a minute you aren't using to meet someone more compatible. This exercise allows you to answer the questions yourself. Once you do, you can stop worrying about what went wrong—and start looking for Mr. or Ms. Right!

1. It wasn't my fault because_____.
2. S/He misunderstood me because_____.
3. S/He said no because of her/his_____.
4. S/He isn't right for me because_____.
5. I'm glad s/he said no because_____.

And now, a final note: getting rejected is a disappointment. Feeling rejected is disappointment turned inward.

Maybe you had hoped that your fledgling liaison would turn to love. Maybe you would have been more than happy to settle for simple lust. Whatever your fantasy, the dream of finding that special someone isn't something any of us should let go of.

But letting go of self-blame, keeping life's disappointments out of your head (and your social interactions) ... those are skills we all can master. Stop accepting and buying destructive emotions that undermine your self-esteem. Reprogram positive thoughts to your negative chatterbox. If a potential partner has given you a case of defensive dater syndrome, give it back. In so doing, you'll be giving yourself a gift: the chance to get on, get out, and get busy looking for a kinder, gentler, more appropriate companion.

THE REJECTION RECAP

Remember:

- ❤ Everybody gets rejected. Tom Selleck was Bachelor Number 2 twice on *The Dating Game* and was never picked.
- ❤ Develop a philosophy of rejection. Don't personalize. It's not you who's being rejected—it's the intimacy.
- ❤ Don't dwell on your most recent no. Move on to the next person.
- ❤ Nobody ever died of a wounded ego. (It just feels that way.)
- ❤ You may be wonderful, but you aren't the Amazing Kreskin. Don't try to read the minds of the people you meet.
- ❤ Flirting is not goal-oriented. Put your serious intentions aside.
- ❤ Don't anticipate the *N* word. Stay in the here and now.
- ❤ Immediate turndowns aren't setbacks. They are opportunities to move forward.
- ❤ Don't spend your life searching for the Hope Diamond. You'll miss all the other gems along the way.
- ❤ Most of all, remember that meeting the right person is a numbers game. All you need is one!

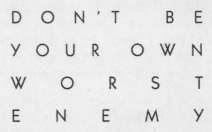

7

DON'T BE YOUR OWN WORST ENEMY

"Every woman's mother tells her that they have to kiss a lot of frogs before one finally turns into a handsome prince. What they don't tell you is how to get rid of the frogs that don't turn into anything. Is there any money in starting a frog farm?" —NANETTE, age 38

"It occurred to me one night after my former girlfriend and I had one of our knock-down drag-outs over—what else?—my jealousy. Well, the argument was getting us nowhere and she grabbed her coat to leave so I yelled after her, 'Isn't that typical? We have a discussion and you run out.' She said, 'That's just it. We aren't having a discussion. You're fighting with yourself.' With that, she left, slamming the door behind her. I didn't go after her. I just sat there

*thinking, 'You know, she's right. I am arguing with myself.
And the worst part is, I'm not winning.'"* —TONY, age 26

He says he'll call but doesn't. She says she'd do anything
for you—and ends up doing unspeakable things *to* you. The
things that other people do to us as flirts, as lovers, and as
friends are confusing, confounding, and often unkind—but
they simply can't compare with the negative mind games
and self-defeating tricks we play on and with ourselves.

Consider the harmless sad sack whom your cousin
(who apparently doesn't really like you) introduced you to
last year. You can't stand the sight of him (not really—you
just aren't crazy about him) but can't bear the thought of
rejecting him. As a result, he's still your every-other-
Saturday-night date, and the only time you're cheerful is on
Monday mornings.

Now consider Tony's plight. His dubious distinction is
that he actually allowed a woman he cared for very much to
dash through the door and out of his life while he and the
pointless, destructive thoughts that turned him into a jeal-
ous fool spent a cozy evening *mano a mano* in his empty
apartment.

I wish I could tell you that these few examples of self-
sabotage were all that I could come up with to justify the
need for this chapter. But they aren't. Nearly every man
and woman who enrolls in my seminar has a story to tell
that puts a new spin on the word "self-downing." And what
it has shown me is that most of us don't need other people
to rain on our parade. We're more than willing to do the
slosh work ourselves. And that would be okay if sacrificing
our self-esteem made us happy. But it doesn't.

Negative thoughts turn into negative action. And
whether you're flirting, working, or working at flirting,
negative action keeps you from doing what you want, ac-
complishing what you must, and getting all you can out of
your social and professional life.

In this chapter, I address the pitfalls that routinely foil the flirting efforts of the singles I know. The first—listening to your negative chatterbox—makes contact with others impossible. The second—a lack of persistence—makes it easy to give up too soon. The third stumbling block is not thinking the possibility is real, and the fourth is the inability to give up on failing relationships soon enough.

Is it possible to slide through the remainder of your single life without confronting these issues? Many people do. But if you truly aspire to becoming a better flirt, you should know that the process begins when you become a better friend to yourself. This chapter enables you not only to identify the pitfalls in your path but also to remove them. Its purpose is to help you *see* yourself as your best ally and to teach you to *treat* yourself that way.

Ready to become a kinder, gentler flirt? Then roll up your sleeves! The breaks that really count are the ones we give ourselves. We'll begin by breaking the negative thinking habit, once and for all.

REPROGRAMMING YOUR NEGATIVE CHATTERBOX

Late one night, I tuned in to a movie whose plot revolved around a character who suddenly developed the ability to read the thoughts of others. Naturally, all the people he encountered were thinking ponderous thoughts. Where I might rack my brain for minutes at a clip just trying to reconstitute the shopping list I misplaced, these people were consumed with plots, threats, seduction, revenge, and all the other exciting things that make B movies what they are. And what they are is fiction.

Now, I'm not claiming any supernatural powers. I don't have the ability to connect telepathically with what's going on in someone else's head. (If I could, I'd be too busy admiring my yacht to write books or see clients.) But I am trained to recognize the negative behavior patterns that are symptomatic of negative thoughts. And I can tell you that there are a lot more people out there mentally rerunning unhealthy, self-defeating thoughts than there are hatching conspiracies or plotting revenge. And as for the seductions? The bad news is that they are usually among the first casualties of a rampant negative chatterbox. The good news is that it really doesn't have to be that way once you become aware of the subliminal static in your head.

WHAT THE CHATTERBOX SOUNDS LIKE

Terry is a recently divorced man in his forties. He confronted his negative chatterbox for the first time a few weeks ago, in the aftermath of a breakup that should have been easy for him.

"It's not that I was particularly attached to Joanne," he explained. "To tell you the truth, I was only dating her because nothing better seemed to be coming my way. Oh, she was a nice enough woman ... but I had no real feelings for her—until she broke the relationship off.

"The way it happened was sort of ironic—even funny. Joanne sat me down and told me all the things I'd been thinking about her! She said that I was a great guy, but we just weren't connecting. I told her that I understood, kissed her on the cheek, and wished her good luck.

"But on my way home, I started wondering what I had done to turn Joanne off. Were my jokes corny? Was my conversation boring? Should I have been more romantic? Less timid? About two days later, my head was so full of questions, I actually called Joanne and asked her whether I'd done anything to offend her! She said no, of course. But now my head is more full of questions than ever."

"I'm not worthy; I'm not valuable; I must have done something wrong." The chatterbox's message is a veritable litany of irrational and destructive beliefs that are repeated constantly throughout our lives. So why do we notice them so seldom? Unfortunately, we've gotten used to them. Our chatterboxes were installed in childhood. By the time we reach adulthood, our own negative messages about our looks, competence, personality, and abilities have become what sound technicians call "white noise"—a dull, atonal background sound that we don't consciously register until, like Terry, we realize that we're acting on it.

Self-deprecation and irrational beliefs are like a dysfunctional parent. They nag at you until you are convinced that you must expect less because you deserve less. But unlike a dysfunctional parent, the negative chatterbox is easily reprogrammed to affirm rather than undermine, to support instead of sabotage. All you need is a basic knowledge of Dr. Albert Ellis's rational-emotive therapy—and a method that is as simple as A, B, C.

A MODEL FOR SELF-SUPPORT

In Chapter 6, I revealed how Albert Ellis applied the principles of his own groundbreaking work to overcome his own feelings of rejection—and how you could do the same. In this chapter, you will learn to use Ellis's ABC model to identify all the situations that *Activate* irrational thinking, change your *Belief* systems for the better, and open the door to happier, more fulfilling emotional *Consequences*. How does the model work? I'll illustrate with a very simple example. A man walks into an elevator. He gets kicked in the leg from behind and he is in pain. That's A. He becomes very angry. That's C. At this point most of us feel that A causes C, or that getting kicked made him angry. But the man turns around and sees that the man who kicked him is blind. He's no longer angry; his feelings of anger are replaced with compassion. Now he may be a little annoyed and hurt, but the fury disappears. Why? If A always caused C, he would stay angry. But we control our A's and C's to the degree we program our B's, or belief systems. Our B is what we tell ourselves and how we perceive a situation. This man in the elevator has an altered B. His new B belief says, "This man did not kick me on purpose nor try to hurt me. In fact, he is blind." He suddenly feels sorry for the man, and realizes it wasn't his fault. His anger subsides and turns to compassion, proving that A does not necessarily lead to C. If we employ rational beliefs, eliminate crooked and magical thinking, and talk ourselves out of our irrational thinking, all our C's will seem less serious.

When Terry came into my office, he immediately identified the A—the activating situation that prompted his emotions—and the C, or emotional consequence of his interaction with Joanne. But the entire scenario didn't come together for him until he saw it on paper, like this:

A: Joanne tells Terry what he already knows: that they have nothing in common and that there are no sparks between them.

C: Terry goes home, where he becomes increasingly upset, self-deprecating, and depressed.

He looked the statements over with a quizzical expression. "This doesn't make sense," he commented finally. "The A statement is accurate—and as much as I hate to admit it, those *are* the emotional consequences I feel. But if the activating situation is supposed to be the reason why I feel so upset, why doesn't the A lead to the C? Something is missing here."

"But that's just it, Terry. The activating situation doesn't lead to the emotional consequence. Your irrational beliefs do. And we haven't gotten to those yet."

"Irrational? Me?" Terry looked at me, perplexed.

"Believe me, it will all come clear," I told him. "But first, let me tell you a story. There are three young women who are each having affairs with married men. Woman number one is lonely and depressed. She wants to call her boyfriend at home and wants to see him when she knows he is spending time with his wife. She feels he *should* call her on weekends and *must* leave his wife if he loves her. Because she hates playing second fiddle, she is miserable and sometimes suicidal.

"The second young woman is a part-time actress who is totally satisfied with the relationship. The man has given her things she would never be able to buy for herself, including a diamond bracelet and a vacation in the Bahamas twice a year. Other than the time she spends with him at swanky hotels, she is free to pursue her theatrical endeavors. She makes no demands and believes the arrangement is perfect.

"Woman number three has an entirely different perspective on the situation. She is neither particularly happy nor sad. She knows there's no future in investing all her time and effort in a relationship with a married man, so in her free time she searches for an unmarried replacement. When she's sure she's found Mr. Right, she has every intention of ending the affair for good.

"So there you have it," I concluded, "three women who have been dealt exactly the same cards—with three totally dissimilar outcomes or consequences. Obviously, their activating situations are the same. But their beliefs—what they think *should* happen or *could* happen to fulfill their expectations—are very different. That's because should's and could's really aren't a part of what *is*."

I could tell from the twinkle in Terry's eye that he had gotten the gist of the story. I grabbed a pencil to complete the scenario.

"Now, think about it. What irrational belief do you hold about the effect that Joanne's decision *should* have on you? What are you telling yourself about the breakup that we haven't written into this chart?"

Terry answered immediately. "That she broke off with me because she found me somehow lacking as a boyfriend. That I could have been a more attentive boyfriend."

"Okay. If that's true, then the whole picture really looks like this."

A: Joanne tells Terry what he already knows: that they have nothing in common and that there are no sparks between them.

B: Terry begins to wonder whether he is somehow responsible for the lack of compatibility. Should he have acted differently? Was he dull? Unromantic?

C: Terry goes home, where he becomes increasingly upset, self-deprecating, and depressed.

"I get it now," said Terry, laying the paper on my desk. "It's my beliefs that make me feel the way I do, not Joanne's bombshell."

Precisely. Terry knew that he and Joanne weren't destined to be the next Romeo and Juliet long before Joanne broke the relationship off. There was no rational reason for him to feel insecure about the breakup—and absolutely no evidence that he had caused it. So where did the self-destructive emotional consequence come from?

Terry's answer was tentative. "My negative chatterbox?"

You bet! I told Terry that if I could tune into the thoughts that formed his irrational beliefs, they would sound something like this:

"Joanne doesn't like me. And Joanne has had a lot of experience with richer, more exciting men. That means that I am not rich enough, exciting enough, or good-looking enough for Joanne or any other woman. I must be doing something wrong or she would find me more appealing."

"That sounds about right," Terry admitted sheepishly. "But you still haven't told me how I can pull the plug on the chatterbox."

I explained to Terry that a negative chatterbox is a perpetual motion machine and that there was no plug to pull. But it was possible for Terry to erase the should's, could's, and must's from his thinking. And it was within his power to dispute the twisted tape loop that reran the negative messages in his head. All he had to do was provide his inner voice with an alternate script—one that reflected rational beliefs rather than the negative static generated by his chatterbox.

He picked up a pencil and wrote this out:

"If Joanne was really so smart, she would know that I was bored with her! So what if she isn't attracted to my type? I'm not attracted to hers! She did me a big favor by breaking the relationship off. I'm relieved that I don't have to make a sham of a partnership work. And I'm glad not to waste too much time on a woman who didn't appreciate me."

To further clarify, Terry's self-talk choices could be diagramed like this:

#1: A	B	C
Joanne tells Terry he has nothing in common with her.	Terry believes he has done wrong and puts himself down.	Anxiety; ego blow; self-downing.

#2: A	B	C
Joanne tells Terry he has nothing in common with her.	Terry is glad to be free. He didn't really want this relationship and was stuck.	It's okay! I feel relieved, happy.

As Shakespeare so succinctly put it, "There is nothing either good or bad, but thinking makes it so." Terry could have chosen to go with his irrational belief (which had as its consequence depression and self-doubt) or with his amended belief, which enabled him to feel relieved at the demise of a dead-end relationship, get on with his life, get on with his flirting, and get out to meet new people.

Of course, many of life's upsets don't resolve themselves quite so neatly. The loss of a job we love, a relationship we depend on, or a partner we truly care about is always accompanied by sadness, disappointment, temporary aimlessness, and slight insecurity. Still, those emotions need not set us back or set us up for full-blown depression. There is a difference between disappointment and devastation. That was the lesson my friend Marci learned when her longtime romance dissolved.

Marci and Ray never married, but they lived together for nearly eleven years. During that time, they shared everything, from the bills and housework to their most intimate secrets. It seemed ironic, then, that Ray's willingness to reveal himself to Marci proved to be the final blow to their relationship. One night, after dinner, Ray confessed that he had had an affair with a paralegal in his law firm. When Marci spoke to me, she said she "hasn't had a moment's peace since."

"Here I was, thinking that the sun rose and set on my perfect lover—and all the while, my darling Raymond was being the perfect lover to someone else! How do you think that makes me feel?" Marci shouted, her voice full of anger. "Like a fool, that's how! Now everybody's telling me that I need to get out of the house—that I need to meet other men. Why? Because I wasn't humiliated enough the first time? Do I need to give the male species another crack at me?"

What Marci needed was to stop taking cracks at herself. Of course, many of her perceptions were right on target. Ray had betrayed her—it was only natural that she felt violated. He had also destroyed Marci's shining image of him—which left Marci feeling disillusioned, even foolish. But although Marci had been willing to release Ray, she hadn't begun to release the residual feelings of anger she harbored toward him. Worse yet, she had begun to direct that anger at all men—and at herself.

When we detailed Marci's situation on the ABC chart, it looked like this:

A: Ray violates Marci's trust in him and her reliance on an eleven-year partnership by having an affair.

B: Marci believes that her love for Ray somehow blinded her to his transgressions. She feels she has been a fool—and will only be fooled again. Men are rotten—who needs them?

C: Marci is angry at Ray for leaving, furious at her friends for suggesting that she get on with her life, and hostile toward all men for their cavalier treatment of the women who love them. Most of all, she feels fearful, lonely, and isolated.

It is difficult to view our own behavior objectively. But when I handed the paper to Marci, she began to see her situation in a different light and to recognize her irrational beliefs. "That woman is a real case, isn't she?" she commented. "I wouldn't even let a person like that be my friend ... and she's me!" As a therapist I helped her dispute her irrational beliefs and re-examine the destructive thinking that was making her miserable.

It was all Marci needed to psych up for the next step. She wrote her alternate script with devilish pleasure.

"B: Marci feels her love for Ray temporarily blinded her to his transgressions. She may have been fooled once, but she learned by the experience."

"And now?"

Marci smiled and shrugged. "I'm still angry," she admitted, "but I've given up eleven years on Ray. There's no sense spending one more going over the details of a relationship that's kaput. And who knows, maybe if I get out of the house once in a while, I'll meet a man with better character and I'll get over the anger altogether. I don't have

Ray to take care of me anymore. So I'll just have to take better care of myself."

And that's what being your own best friend is all about: taking care of yourself as well as others—making sure that the messages you send inward are as considerate and uplifting as the ones you send out into the external world.

In rational-emotive therapy, I've found a workable method for putting my negative chatterbox to rest. And if you add the D, or the dispute, to the ABC model, RET becomes a self-help paradigm that you can apply to your negative-thinking patterns and hopefully eliminate some of your most frequent irrational beliefs—the *shoulds, musts, and demands* we all place on ourselves and others, and the belief that we need to be perfect in this imperfect world. It would also help us to be kinder to ourselves if we accepted that we are all "fallible human beings," and do not have to be loved and accepted by everyone, all the time, even though that would be nice.

The D, or dispute, is a testing, probing technique you can use to question your irrational beliefs. Ask yourself, How do I know this is so? Where is it written? What would be the worst thing that could happen? Is this a proven fact? Create a dialogue with yourself that examines what you are telling yourself and what it is based on. Is it sensible to believe that because he finds me unattractive, all men do? Nonsense. Because my last relationship failed, I am a failure? Wrong. Remember those times when he or she thought you were hot stuff and the many times you succeeded and had a fine romance.

If we could apply some of the principles of RET, we might be able to modify our extreme feelings and replace depression with sadness, devastation with disappointment, and anger with annoyance. The latter of each set of emotions are healthier and less self-defeating and allow us to act to solve our problems instead of dwelling or being paralyzed by them.

In the ABCD model, you will find a positive technique that enables you to get beyond life's negative turns, and take full advantage of my next guideline for happy flirting...

TRY, TRY AGAIN

The change in Livvie, a woman in my seminar, was like the difference between night and day. The first week, she left the classroom with a cheery good-bye and an energetic spring in her step. At our next meeting, she could hardly look at me. After class, I asked what was the matter.

"To tell you the truth, Susan, I wasn't even going to come tonight," she confessed. "You see, I did what you said to do. On the way home from class, I stopped off a local pub—and I made eye contact with a guy I'd seen there before. At first, he sort of smiled at me so I sent over a drink. Next thing you know, he's right in my face saying thanks but no thanks and I'm hoping someone's cigarette starts a fire so I can run screaming out into the street without being noticed."

"Wait a minute," I said. "You're leaving something out here. Why did he say he didn't want the drink?"

Livvie waved her hand as though she was trying to make me disappear. "I don't know! First he said something about having to drive to his parents' house, then he said something about the time...but what difference does it make? I'm just not a natural flirt. And I'm never going to make a fool of myself like that again. Never, *ever*."

If Livvie hadn't anticipated rejection, she would have realized that her new acquaintance was turning down a drink—not the opportunity for a friendly chat. And if she had tuned into the tenor of the exchange, she would have realized that the man was asking her to try again on a more laid-back night—not telling her to give up on flirting forever.

Unfortunately, Livvie made good on her threat. She withdrew from the class and, as far as I know, from becoming a fully functioning member of single society. The class missed her—and I'm willing to bet that the man at the bar did, too.

In this book, I've described single life as a continuing journey, full of interesting twists and turns. In my mind, the road to happiness has detours rather than dead ends, alternate routes rather than roadblocks. That's why it upsets me when I encounter self-defeating singles like Livvie who put up signs that read, "last chance for flirting," or, "wrong way—go back," into the scenario.

Flirting is not a direct route to marriage, bed, or any other destination you have in mind. You simply can't expect to get where you're going on the first try—or even the second. So what if that handsome brute turns down your invitation to dance? Ask him whether he'd rather join you in a game of pinball or share a slice of pizza. And what about that promising Ms. who tells you she'll call and doesn't? You've got a phone book. Use it! Give her a call. Or call someone else. Just don't give up on flirting! That will surely get you nowhere.

By the way, the saying goes, "Try, try again," not "Try, try, try, and *try*, until the object of your flirtation is forced to hire bodyguards to keep you away!" We have all known people who hated each other the first few times they met but somehow went on to become latter-day Adams and Eves, turning the world into their private Garden of Eden, repopulating the earth with rosy-cheeked children. But we have also known suitors who simply couldn't—or wouldn't—take no for an answer, no matter how clearly we expressed our lack of interest.

There is a fine line between persistence and pestering, and although the exact placement of that line may be diffi-

cult to ascertain, the second no is a good place to start. After all, you've let that special person know—not once, but
twice—that you're interested. If he or she isn't looking
your way, smiling in your direction, or making any moves
to approach you, you're wasting your time. Try, try again—
this time with a more discerning single.

DO YOU REALLY WANT HIM OR HER?

Sexual attraction or chemistry is a powerful and motivating
force for action, but some of us choose not to move beyond
that secret crush. Why? That was the topic that I was invited to discuss on the Montel Williams Show, as four people revealed their secret attraction to four unsuspecting
crushees to a studio audience and millions of people across
the nation.

A crush is an infatuation, which is defined as "an in-
tense and foolish love and admiration." Now, I am not saying that infatuation is always foolish, but it is usually based
on fantasy rather than reality. We rarely know the person
well and might have simply seen them across a crowded
room or on a bus. Yet we attribute all kinds of inviting, exciting traits to this person. Being smitten with a co-worker
or schoolmate, idolizing a teacher or superior without
knowing much about this object of our love is the essence
of infatuation. Infatuation is characterized by euphoria,
daydreaming about this person, and imagining her or him
all day long. We can become restless, preoccupied, sleep-
less, anxious. We wait for the telephone to ring and include
this person in all our plans, picturing them every day in every way. The rush is sensational, and we are in a constant
state of excitation. It is no wonder many of us get stuck
and want to remain there. But if you want to find out if this
person is interested in you too and could become a date or
mate, it is necessary to act on the fantasy.

Why does she admire his biceps at the health club and

never say a word? Why does he stare at her in biology class every day and run out at the bell before she gets up from her desk? Why does he send love notes unsigned, and why does she hang up on his answering machine? The reasons are varied. Maybe it is shyness, fear of rejection, terror at commitment, enjoyment of fantasy, or he or she may find forbidden fruit more desirable and never want to find out the truth about the person.

Whatever the reason for not acting on a secret crush, attraction for all of us is very real. Psychologists tell us sexual chemistry is based on love maps. We are attracted to people in our present who remind us of people we cared for in our past. Those love objects usually appeared at a vulnerable time of our lives such as puberty or when we were insecure or separated from home. Biologists will attribute sexual attraction to pheromones, the scents responsible for mating in the animal kingdom—surely the perfume industry believes this. Whatever the cause, and I certainly wish I had the answer, we do know that sexual chemistry, attraction, and crushes are aided by mystery, barriers, timing, loneliness, unavailability, and the fact that like usually attracts like. Those factors are important in flirting, and add to your appeal in beginnings. In fact, when you become a little mysterious, slightly distant, and have less time for someone than he or she desires, you add a certain extra appeal to your assets. It is human nature that we want what we can't have.

However, if you are limiting your socializing to fantasy, crushes, and infatuations that go nowhere, I suggest that you take a risk. Controlled risk taking is crucial to flirting, and by indicating to that person that you have an interest in him you up your chances 100 percent of making a connection. Send a rose to her lunch table (this time sign the card), write him a note and sail it over on a paper airplane, hand her a calling card asking to meet her, place post-its in his desk drawer with pleasant messages, or just invite her to lunch, coffee, or the movies. See if there is more to this person than what you imagined. Maybe he is better than your wildest dreams—or a true dud. Find out if she could be interested in you as well. You may get rejected, your bubble may burst, but then when you get over that (refer to Chapter 6), you will be able to go on with your life, free yourself for the opportunity of finding someone worthwhile who will reciprocate your feelings, and flirt, date, and perhaps mate with a real person—not a foolish fantasy.

WHEN YOU DON'T WANT THE ONE WHO WANTS YOU

At a cocktail party, you've met a man who has all the makings of your handsome prince, but as soon as he opens his mouth, he says something that makes you want to croak. Or perhaps you've been dating that woman you wanted to know better—and now that you do, you know better than to continue the relationship. How do you handle sticky situations like these? Unfortunately, if you're like most of us, you don't.

Mary was a friend I met a work. And although our relationship was temporary (like the job!), one conversation we shared will stay with me forever. It took place just before Mary left on a two-week vacation. I asked where she was going to spend her time off.

"First, I'm going upstate to meet Charles's parents," she reported without enthusiasm. "After a few days, the two of us will catch a flight to the Bahamas."

"You're what?" I choked. "But Mary, I thought you couldn't stand Charles!"

My friend shrugged. "I can't—but that doesn't mean I want to hurt his feelings."

I speak to hundreds of men and women every year, and the variations I've heard on the "I-don't-love-him-but-I-can't-leave-him" theme are endless. Even my seminars—

which I've geared specifically to people who are *un*at-tached—are teeming with men and women who simply can-not make the break: men who stay because they "don't like to see women cry"; women who string men along until someone better appears; and singles of both sexes who can't take rejection—and can't dish it out, either.

You may feel that you have "good reasons" for keeping the wrong company. But are those reasons so good? Not if you want to be fair to yourself—and a good friend to your partner! Tying yourself to an inappropriate relationship not only puts you in bondage, but it keeps your partner from seeking a more compatible mate. While you may convince yourself that you're doing him or her a favor by delaying the inevitable, in reality your procrastination is wasting two people's time, making two people unavailable to others, and keeping both of you from attracting more suitable com-panionship.

Don't settle for crumbs when you can have the whole loaf! I know that rejecting others isn't easy. Doing it with grace requires courage and skill. Since flirting is a risk you have successfully taken, you know you have the courage. As for the skill, the techniques I outline below will help. They enable you to say no nicely but firmly, to be kind to yourself, and to stay on the good side of your soon-to-be ex. And why is it so important that you stay friends with Mr. or Ms. Not-Quite-Right? Because friends are the basis of great social networks—and large, diverse networks make for great flirting!

So how do you unload a relationship that isn't working without taking on a load of guilt?

Use "I" messages. Beginning every sentence of your adieu speech with the word "you" (as in, "You just aren't right for me," or "You just can't keep quiet during a movie and it drives me crazy!") places the blame for the failed re-lationship squarely on your partner's shoulders—and that makes for hurt feelings.

Since you are the one who has diagnosed the incompatibility, it is important that you admit your feelings and take responsibility for your actions. Make a conscious effort to use "I" messages, such as, "I feel we have nothing in common," or "I'm not looking for commitment right now." Although I can't promise that this technique will make the situation painless, it will leave your partner's ego intact. And that will help any residual wounds to heal faster.

To be sweet, be brief. If you've ever been on the receiving end of a breakup speech that turned into a historical analysis of your sins, failures, and inadequacies (and who hasn't?), you'll understand the merciful intent behind this suggestion.

Keep your no's simple and to the point. And for heaven's sake, stay in the here and now. Simply say, "I feel_____," and move on.

Cushion the blow by saying something positive before or after you drop the bombshell. It'll make the impact of your message that much more bearable.

Can't think of anything nice to say to that creep who monopolized the shank of your evening—or the best years of your life? Then think back to what intrigued you about that person in the first place. Say, for instance, "I love the way you express your ideas, but I really feel we're not connecting." Then smile (Why not? The whole encounter is about to become a memory!) and hit the flirting trail.

Remember that you are not responsible for another person's reaction. It can be very difficult to disengage from someone else's pain—particularly if that someone has been an important part of your life. But breaking off means separating yourself physically and emotionally from a relationship that is unfulfilling. Until you do, neither of you will be able to move on to more productive liaisons.

Your partner's tears can't wash away the reasons for your unhappiness. And your partner's arguments will never rationalize the basis for your decision out of existence. If the going gets tough, remind yourself that a relationship gone wrong can't always be righted. And don't allow your determination to crumble. That merely buys time—and it doesn't take long for an inappropriate relationship to become even more unpleasant, perhaps even destructive.

Accept that you will not be universally loved. In your fantasies you may be the darling of every man, woman, child, and beast that ever walked, crawled, or slithered on the earth. In reality, even Santa Claus, the Easter Bunny, and Julie Andrews have their detractors. So why go on beating yourself up and putting yourself down for not winning the unconditional admiration of everyone you meet?

Doing what you have to do—even if you take great pains to do it gently—will bring you more flak than appreciation. The only consolation is that doing what everyone else wants you to do will generally work out the same way!

If your decision to end a liaison leaves your partner with bad feelings about you, so be it. Time will tell whether that animosity will eventually pass. Meanwhile, you have every reason to feel good about your honesty, your empathy, and your future.

Close the conversation with kindness. I don't believe that there's ever a good reason to add insult to injury by treating others with rudeness, sarcasm, or hostility. As the song says, "Breaking Up Is Hard to Do." Working out your unresolved anger in the last ten minutes you spend together just makes it harder.

Deliver your message clearly but with empathy. If you're sorry about the way the relationship is ending, say so. If not, at least let your ex know that you empathize with his or her pain.

And for everyone's sake, don't say you'll call if you know you won't. That isn't an act of kindness—it's an act of cowardice.

CLEANING HOUSE

I have a friend who gets through any bad times that befall her by cleaning out her closets. Granted, there are more hedonistic routes of escape—like a round-the-world cruise on the *QE II*. And nearly any therapeutic option is less dusty. Still, my friend's unique style of self-help not only provides her with an opportunity for catharsis, it also gives her time to think about the lifestyle she envisions for herself, and to discard all the old, worn-out items and ideas that just don't seem to fit that image.

To me, this chapter is closet-cleaning day for the date-and-relate set. It is my hope that the advice I've given here will help you eliminate the negative thoughts that have accumulated throughout your single life, to give self-blame the heave-ho once and for all, and to throw out all the self-defeating behaviors that no longer fit the confident, compassionate flirt you have become.

And who knows ... you may meet a significant other who wants to store a few personal objects in your closet— now that you have the room!

HOW TO TREAT YOURSELF WITH TLC

Remember:

- The things that others do to us can't compare to the things we do to ourselves. Ease up! You're your own best asset!
- To tune out your negative chatterbox, tune into the ABC model.
- "There is nothing either good or bad, but thinking makes it so." Don't let irrational beliefs color your view of the world.
- Question everything! To dispute a destructive belief is to defeat it.

- ❤ Flirting is not a one-shot deal. Try, try again!
- ❤ Don't be *too* persistent. Nobody likes a pest.
- ❤ There are no good reasons for keeping the wrong company. Move on to more suitable companionship and let Mr. or Ms. Not-Quite-Right do the same.
- ❤ If you have the courage to flirt, you have what it takes to say no nicely. Use "I" messages. Don't attack others.
- ❤ You are not responsible for anyone else's reaction. Be brief, be polite, then be on your way.
- ❤ Be your own best friend! Test out your infatuation and don't let yourself settle for crumbs when you could have the whole loaf!

Now you're ready! I am confident that the techniques and exercises in this book have helped you to make the most of your natural talents and to sharpen the special skills that make it easy to date, relate, and meet a potential mate. But where to begin? *Remember this is a numbers game.* The more people you interact with the better your chances of meeting that "significant other."

These are just a sampling of the happy hunting grounds that have worked for me, my friends, and the 2,500 successful flirts who have attended my workshops and lectures. If you pick and choose among them, I'm sure you'll find an environment to complement your unique brand of flirting. But if you're adventurous, you can simply work your way down the list. Remember, to flirt you must *approach*, have the right *attitude*, and take *action*. These are the Three A's you need to get on your flirting report card in order to attract anyone, anytime, anyplace. After all, you can attract anyone you choose—and the best setting for that is anyplace you are! Are you ready? Go!

SUGGESTED PLACES TO MEET

Acting classes
Adult education classes
Aerobics classes
Animal rights groups
Antiques shows
Art gallery openings
Auctions
Ballroom dance classes
Bicycling clubs
Book discussion groups
Bridge, backgammon, or chess clubs
Charity functions
Churches and synagogues
Classical-music-lovers' groups
Club Meds
Coffee shops
Comedy club tryouts
Comic-book conventions
Community organizations
Computer classes
Cooking classes
Concerts
Conventions
Craft fairs
Cross-country ski tours
Dating services
Dances
Discussion groups and seminars
Ecological groups
Financial seminars
Flea markets
Fund-raisers
Garage sales
Garden tours

Gyms
Hardware stores
Hiking tours and clubs
Hotel lobbies (ask for a restaurant recommendation)
Jewelry designing classes
Jury duty
Language classes
Lectures
Library discussion groups
Magazines of special interest
Marathons and sporting events
Museums
Mushroom-lovers' society (yes, there is one)
New Age conferences and workshops
New cities (ask directions!)
Newspapers (check for singles events)
Outdoor clubs
Parents Without Partners (or other single-parent groups)
Parks and recreation areas
Parties (throw one!)
Personal ads
Playgrounds (borrow a kid if you have to!)
Poetry readings
Political organizations
Pool halls (upscale, please)
Racquetball or squash tournaments
Real estate seminars
Restaurants
Reunions
Sailing (book yourself on a charter)
Scenic overlooks (ask that interesting stranger to take your
     picture!)
Sculpture classes
Sierra Club meetings
Singles organizations
Ski-lift lines and ski lodges

Spas
Sporting events
Street fairs
Support groups
Tennis parties
Trade shows
Theater clubs
Walking tours
Walking your dog
Weddings
Weight-loss support groups
White-water rafting
Wine-tastings
Zoos (they bring out the playful animal in everyone)

Good luck!

AUTHOR'S NOTE

Susan Rabin hopes you laughed, learned, and enjoyed her book. If you are interested in purchasing her audio cassette, "How to Flirt, Date, and Meet Your Mate," please enclose $13.00 (which includes postage) to:

Susan Rabin
Gracie Station
P.O. Box 660
New York, NY 10028

She is also available for lectures and seminars.